A Microphone is Not the Muzzle of a Gun

INTERVIEWING SKILLS:

Tips & Techniques
for Conducting
or Facing
a Wide Range of
Interviews

A Microphone is Not the Muzzle of a Gun

INTERVIEWING SKILLS:

Tips & Techniques
for Conducting
or Facing
a Wide Range of
Interviews

Rusty LaGrange

A Microphone is Not the Muzzle of a Gun

printed and distributed

by

Rusty's Rose Enterprises, Publishing

A Division of
A Flair for Words
copywriting and consulting
www.aFlairForWords.com
P.O. Box 1002, Lucerne Valley, CA 92356
Copyright 2019

Reproducing any or all parts of this book—or distributing it electronically—is prohibited by international and U.S.A. copyright laws and treaties, and would subject the purchaser to penalties of up to $100,000 PER COPY distributed. Permission to reprint must be approved by the author.

ISBN: 978-1092395328

~~ DEDICATION ~~

To "Red"

When I first sat down to begin gathering my thoughts for this book, I drummed up wonderful memories of the first days of my journalism career. Then I found myself thinking back to the earlier days of high school, when I wrote for my school paper.

I wasn't thinking of the power of it at that time. I was focused on sharing. I wanted the news I wrote to enlighten and inform. I wrote short stories for my amusement and poetry for my soul. But, mostly, I had to write the news.

At age 16 I came across a retired police detective who spent weekends at the San Jose Flea Market, housed in a big red barn renovated for that purpose. My dad and I were selling used furniture and kitchen appliances that my dad had repaired. I really did enjoy my three-month summer break spent selling with my dad and talking to the older sellers. I kept a journal of my days and kept my craft honed on recording conversations among the venders.

That's when I met Ira "Red" Simpson, who garnered an academic yet nurturing atmosphere around him. He had experienced so much death and disillusionment during his lifelong career as a police officer that he just wanted to find real people to talk to. He didn't want his conversations to be muddied by his craft of interrogation. He just wanted to be around nice folks.

I found his affability to be genuine. He made me want to ask more questions about his wife and family, his sons' narrow escapes as second-generation officers, and more. However, Red was a tired, old man: overweight, known to sip from a bottle, and nearing 80. He had watery eyes of smoky blue and a bulbous nose, tinged in pink, set in a wide, round face. If he'd had hair and a beard, he could have easily doubled for Santa.

He also had a propensity for falling asleep in the middle of a conversation. When he woke up a few minutes later, he would apologize and explain that he had learned how to "catch a doze" whenever he could while he was a beat cop in Boston. The practice sort of backfired on him in his later years. He could snooze at the drop of a hat. I had to be on my best game and keep the conversation going as I interviewed him before he lapsed into a "doze." Our subjects of conversation ranged widely; he always had an opinion. A true Bostonian Democrat.

His items for sale ranged from glass bric-a-brac to books to musical instruments. I eyed the guitar he brought in one day. He said it was an f-hole jazz guitar with a convex face made from tiger's eye maple, crafted by Kay Guitars. Kay was known to flood the market with cheap guitars to sell to the students who wanted to "learn guitar in 3 weeks." I didn't care who made it. I wanted it. Then Red taught me the true meaning of patience and aiming for a goal. I could have the guitar at a rock bottom price if I made some signs for his booth.

We struck a deal.

Weeks later I walked out owning the Kay Guitar for $16 and two of Dad's kitchen chairs. Red got four hand-painted signs for his booth. I learned from him that the good conversationalist holds a gamut of truths and lies, stories and fabrications, gems and fool's gold. It takes a good ear to hear the truth in a person's voice, an eye to watch body language, personal insight to grasp the essence—and experience to know the difference.

~~ ACKNOWLEDGMENTS ~~

As I approached my book idea, I gathered the names of people who had recently made a profound difference in my writing skills and style, my interviewing techniques, and in my placement of chapters and their topics ... the aesthetics of how this book came together.

I owe a great deal to the new friendships I've developed while compiling the book, as well as those who read and critiqued my work to make it what it has become. As my book came together, I also realized how much help had been offered through the friendships established in my nine-year association with L.V. Writers' Ink, a writers support group in my hometown of Lucerne Valley, and four years in my critiquing group through the High Desert branch of the California Writers Club.

A big "thank you" goes to those CWC members, including: Carol Warren, Virginia Hall, Jenny and John Margotta, Mike Raff, Linda Cooper, Diane Neil, Barbara Badger, Anthony Enriquez, Jan Terry, and others who attended through our past year together. I also wish to note the support and information provided through other members-at-large: 2012 Branch President Bob Isbill, Naomi Ward, Angela Horn, Madeline Gornell, Mary Scott, and Roberta Smith.

This book is dedicated to Red and the CWC critique members for their encouragement, insight, and valuable feedback. Their ideas for fleshing out my chapters to include body language, and new authors marketing their books in an unfamiliar environment, make this product worthy of an enjoyable read. Thanks for your invaluable influence.

I chose Jenny Margotta as my manuscript editor. She's completed over 90 book editing assignments and is most capable when the book finally needs to be on the shelf

I should also mention that I owe so much to my mom who, in those early years, let me stay up well past my bedtime to write poetry in front of the hall heater until I could barely keep my eyes open. She knew the Muse is a great enabler and should be catered to with sufficient time to allow the creativity to flow. Moms are like that ... loving everything you do, in spite of yourself.

~ Rusty

~~ TABLE OF CONTENTS ~~

INTRODUCTION i
1. THE INTERVIEW ~~ 1
   An Atmosphere of Ease 2
   Witty Subjects 5
   Informative Details 6
   A Sense of Style 7
2. THE BETTER INTERVIEW 11
   Practice Takes Effort 12
   Question and Answer Format 13
   Story Format 17
   Case Study Format 20
   Table of Contents Format 21
3. THE POLICE INTERVIEW 23
   Under Duress 23
   Man on the Street 25
   Hard News Reporting 26
4. WHY SOME INTERVIEWS SHINE 31
   Stories Sell 32
   Seven Darn Good Reasons
      Why You Should Tell Me a Story 36
   When Your Subject Works the Room 39
   The Confident Subject 40
   The Exclusive Interview 44
5. EVERYONE HAS A STORY TO SHARE 51
   The Ghostwriter 51
   The Expert 56
   The Wannabe 57

    The Success Story 57
    The Failure Story 58
    The Survival Story 60
    It's Not About You 61
6. TRICKS OF THE TRADE 63
    It's Okay If You Sweat 63
    First Level: Newspaper, Regional News 64
    Second Level: Magazine or Book 64
    Third Level: TV, Web Camera 64
    Hire an Actor 66
    Working from Notes 67
    Winging It 68
7. FOLLOW THE TRENDS 69
    Technology: The Ever-Changing Frontier 69
    Catching Those Tricky Airwaves 70
    33 RADIO INTERVIEW TIPS FOR AUTHORS 71
    Podcasts, Webcasts, and Skype 77
    Blogging and Social Media 79
8. THE JOB INTERVIEW 81
    Act As If You Do … 81
9. LIE TO ME 89
    The Science of Body Language 89
    Body Parts 92
    Fodder for Assessment 94
    Job Interview Tips 95
    Emotional Expressions 96
10. AUTHOR, TAKE THE STAGE 101
    The Brand 101
    The Book Buyer and Sales Etiquette 103
    Who Are You? 105
11. PACKAGED TO SELL 107

 Travel Every day 108
12. THE GIFT IN YOUR HAND 113
 The Next Step is You 115
BONUS: The Gift in Your Hand: Microphone Etiquette 117
BONUS: Microphone 101 119
NOTES 123
REFERENCES 125
ABOUT THE AUTHOR 127

"The greatest part of a writer's time is spent in reading, in order to write: a man will turn over half a library to make one book."

~from *A Book About a Thousand Things*
Samuel Johnson
English poet, essayist
1709 - 1784

~~ INTRODUCTION ~~

When I first became aware of my ease in interviewing people around me, I was about six. I could ask questions without being a nagging, precocious child. Adults always commented how grown up I was. I never recall saying, "Why, why, why," in a whining voice like many children do. I was a listener, an intent listener. There is a true skill in interviewing a subject. Some people struggle with it for years. Some avoid it completely. Some break into a cold sweat just thinking about it. I suppose some come by it naturally.

Now that I've been in the work force for many years and have seen the agony of some authors, students of journalism, and broadcast production people who never felt comfortable approaching the art of interviewing, it appeared that a book was due. Plenty of reference books on this subject sit on the shelves of public libraries and private colleges. Over time, however, new ideas and techniques allow a seasoned interviewer to share insights; a beginning interviewer may come to realize new, as well as time-tested, concepts. So it is that a book about technique would be useful—if not a consoling tool to fall back on—and a solid resource to bolster the person who needs encouragement to tackle the dread of the interview.

My ultimate focus is to help you master early techniques as you learn how elements of an interview come together. It's not just sticking a microphone in someone's face and badgering them until they speak. Believe me, a microphone is not the muzzle of a gun. And if you are confronted with a microphone in your face, maybe you'll fall back on what you've read here and suddenly find yourself gracefully enjoying the moment rather than melting into a pool of jelly.

A good interviewer will learn from the material he receives, will coax attitude and character from his subject while providing compelling information to share, and ultimately, provide entertainment or educational value to his audience.

Throughout this book, I will also cite some talented interviewers' nuggets of advice to help you as they did me. You'll notice the difference in style and poise, tone and topic, discrimination and focus. In your daily life, you'll be more aware of each interview you hear that may be missing the quality, the focus, the charisma that defines a great moment. As you gain understanding in the techniques, you'll also find yourself cringing when you hear an interview spiraling down the drain.

Technology and technique are changing constantly. What is common now may not be in ten years. This I found true when researching many of the topics for this book. I hope this collection of techniques gives access to immediate knowledge of the subject of interviewing without being as overwhelming as other, past books on the subject. Nevertheless, as with the spoken language, interviewing continues to be the most dynamic communication device we have to tell our story or to tell someone else's story.

For any goal, practice and listening to great interviews will enhance your ear for quality, just as a music student learns to hear pitch and tone. I hope, in time, you'll look forward to interviewing someone with the vitality and charm that enables you to shine as you ask the right questions you knew were just waiting to be asked.

~ B.A. Rusty LaGrange, August 2018
Lucerne Valley, CA

~~ 1. THE INTERVIEW ~~

*"Good research, good listening, and finding that hook.
That's what makes a good interview."*

~ Michael Senoff
www.HardtoFindInterviews.com

One on one. It's the joy in capturing a series of conversations that you've guided and researched, becoming the expert record of fact into eternity ...well, into the future anyway. Something notable the general public can access, a specific group may desire, or that can entertain with compelling conversation ... that's the goal of a good interview.

The words are smooth and authoritative, engaging and intelligent, and worthy of the paper they're written on. Your words become tangible and readily shared. Whether in a magazine article read by a traveling CEO on a redeye from Chicago or a homemaker enjoying the conversation on her iPod while her child is taking an afternoon nap, access to information—valuable, timely information—is highly sought after.

Some people can't interview to save their lives. They attempt to follow notes and fumble through them like a teenage boy facing a bra strap on his first date. Anxious, nervous, and fearful, an interviewer can't get to first base until his interviewee is comfortable with him or at least at ease enough to help him move the interview along.

Nothing is more excruciating than a grindingly slow, halting, boring, and embarrassing attempt. Your subject is probably aching to leave the building. Interviewers must learn and grow as they go. It takes practice, but a comfortable and entertaining interview can be engaging. Plan ahead. Think of your ultimate goal: the better you become, the better your choice of guest subjects.

Anyone can learn to interview and make the process enjoyable, interesting, compelling, and worthy of achieving. This book will give you the tools and guidance to help make learning how to interview much easier than that first date or the first time you had to face your classmates during public speaking exercises. The best elements of conducting an interview are comprised of an atmosphere of ease, witty subjects from which to glean entertaining and informative details, and a sense of style that helps the interviewed person drop his guard enough to bring our world into his. Time flies, thoughts are embraced, and a memory is archived.

An Atmosphere of Ease

Choosing the location to conduct an interview will be one of the major elements of controlling the give and take of an interview. However, the location is probably the hardest to orchestrate, due to the flexibility—or lack thereof—of your guest, the time constraints, the restrictions of their location, and even the time of day.

If you're interviewing someone at their home, let them suggest a good place that provides comfort for both of you. Have a glass of water nearby and a box of tissues. Be sure to bring a handy clipboard with you for a solid writing surface. No one wants to fumble with writing on a pillow or knee. Be prepared.

If they are coming to your home or office, the same techniques apply. Try to find a place that is less distracting and quiet. If you use a portable digital recorder, let your subject know in advance—and bring extra batteries.

If you are conducting an impromptu interview, such as a live report, man-on-the-street survey, or an outdoor sports-related event, the elements are going to interrupt, no matter how well you plan. Sprinklers will go on. Heavy traffic will race by. Low flying planes will drown you out. Press forward and take good notes, and be sure to thank the interviewee for his time and patience.

Many first-time interviewees will innocently become stage-struck. It happens to the best of them. Where do you think "deer-in-the-headlights look" came from?

The easiest way to avoid a one-sided conversation with a very shy, nearly numb subject is to ask questions that force a verbal answer. Never ask questions that give the subject the easy out of answering just "yes" or "no." Always frame your questions with more depth and relevancy to coax a verbal comeback.

We've all experienced that awkward moment in a conversation when neither party knows how to continue the verbal exchange. You can avoid this numbing silence by making sure the questions you ask can't be easily answered by a simple one word utterance. On the other hand, if the person keeps responding to your questions in one- or two-word answers, smile and say, "Hmmm, that's interesting. Why do you feel that way?" (from www.workingsolo.com online resources)

Sometimes, the level of conversation turns so intellectual that the interviewer has a hard time keeping up. In this case, your subject has manipulated you into a realm of understanding that he's comfortable in. It will careen out of control until you use the emergency brake. It's up to you to redirect him into speaking in a layman's perspective and a more intuitive understanding of the topic so you both can proceed, and you don't lose your audience.

You might suggest: "Wow. Your industry has a huge collection of words even I haven't heard of before. Can you explain what (blank) means?"

That should give the subject a moment to pause and "dumb down" his selection of industry jargon. Some folks just don't think about how their levels of mastery sound to the layperson. You need to remind them.

One of the benefits of interviewing technical professionals is to pare down their high-powered words into nuggets of information that can be understood at different reading levels and by different audiences. Technical writers are those who extrapolate the meanings of high concept and make them palatable for their bosses to grasp. Yeah, I know it sounds dumb, but are you aware of how many CEOs who, unless they are given the insight and language to make it all user-friendly, have no idea what their engineering employees are producing? A chasm of content definition divides the two factions.

Interviewing a technical-scientific-engineering-type person is one of the hardest undertakings to accomplish. Getting them to relax is even tougher.

If you are interviewing in front of a camera, lighting, seating, and décor can often help the subject to relax and appear more comfortable than he truly is. One of the current celebrities of film and TV, George Cluny, does not give interviews, at least not often. Getting him to appear at ease would be one of the toughest jobs in the world. Once captured, he can be seen ducking, fidgeting, rubbing his hair, and seemingly irritable with each question posed to him. Although he'll flash an irresistible smile, his body language tells us he's ready to run. For an actor of his caliber, he resonates pure fear and excruciating fits of fleeing without leaving his seat. He's a shy star. However, when he's acting, his ability to become at ease and guide you into his make-believe world for 120 minutes is phenomenal.

Finding ways to get your subject to relax is a skill of its own. One process that falls directly on the interviewer is his capacity to engage the subject without causing nervousness, hostility, or even aloofness. The more you gain experience talking and listening, the more comfortable your subject will become.

Start by interviewing a family member, a close friend, or someone at work. See if you can interview someone in the community who is easy to talk to, has a story to tell, and doesn't mind sharing what he knows. Offer your written interview to your local newspaper as a guest commentary or a free column of interest. If you have several interviews planned and in print, offer them to your local paper as a series. Your confidence will help make your next subject relax even more.

Witty Subjects

Part of the challenge of selecting a good subject to interview can be conveyed through the subject's own wit. Someone open to talking, willing to share details of his life, his goals, his viewpoint, and a good sense of humor that comes across easily can be the epitome of a great interview. His own charisma can carry the conversation. He can prompt new questions for you like pulling the information out of a magician's hat. With an interview rolling along, peppered with laughs, clever or satisfying tales, and a demeanor that makes listeners smile, it will be up to you to direct the conversation to a clever end. Maybe prompting the subject to recount one last story before you conclude will be just the reminder he needs to know you are still in control.

Another aspect of a good interviewer is to draw out informative details. A bland but verbose interview is still bland. Many years ago on TV a regional travel-and-interview expert would pick up a telephone book, rummage through it, and randomly point to a name. He would then call the person, make an appointment to go to his home or office, and interview him. He was convinced that everyone had a story to tell, some significance in their lives that others would enjoy learning about. He was right. We joined him in his car as he led us to the subject's home. He studied the area, the curb appeal, and noted significant things that could be used as prompts. As the interview proceeded, we learned unusual tidbits of information. We felt at ease and wondered how many other people might hold personal stories close to their hearts and might want to share. When the interview concluded, we were more than satisfied that we had gained more than he gave.

Week after week he found average people from small towns across the nation willing to tell him a bit of their life. Some were extremely awkward and felt no one could be interested in anything they had accomplished. Yet week by week he never let us down. We learned about a middle-aged waitress who survived cancer and raised two adopted children from overseas; a man who collected dated nails from the railroads and organized the first museum for his collection; and other just as interesting. The thrill was in the details. We learned of twins separated at birth who had just found each other living a few miles apart. People sitting in their living rooms could find deep connections with "average Joes" and be amused and inspired by what they had conquered.

An interview done correctly will enhance people's lives in ways they aren't aware of. "Value-added" is a buzz word term in use today. Conducting an interview with all the elements of a great moment will create an interview that becomes value-added. And value is what will define an interview that lives on for generations.

Informative Details

Capturing a smile as the interviewee tells a tale is like watching a child opening a gift. Whoever is watching the interview will suddenly be enchanted by that smile, and their awareness of their children playing in the next room will fall away, creating a zone of interest and a level of attention that is focused and stimulating. A beguiling smile claims the gauzy territory between raw-edged reality and suspension of disbelief. A fiction writer aims for a reader to fall into their clutches and put aside all connections with the real world, while an interviewer hopes for a one-on-one intensity that fine-tunes the audience to deflect reality for a few minutes.

I mention smile and laughter because they denote true connectivity with a subject. It's very difficult to fake a realistic chuckle or a belly laugh. Also, the depth of story, co-mingled with detail, provides the audience a scope of understanding that anchors them to the current topic. The same can be true for a string of drivers who come across flares on the side of the road, flashing lights a quarter mile away, and the eventual crash scene. We linger and look for the details that verify our existence and our eventual demise in the future. It's a ghoulish scene, but we are in the "now," and details often become exaggerated for our macabre entertainment.

A good interviewer's goal is the "lookie lou"—someone willing to commit to listening and appreciating the conversation, looks forward to the friendly chatter mixed with riveting details that make it become more true, and becomes immersed in them. We look for connectivity and comparison in everything we do.

A Sense of Style

When it comes down to the essence of a good interview, the majority of those that retain a sense of style will remain in your mind much longer than most details. Not that style is your only litmus test to qualify the interview, but style stands as the better value over time.

Yet style itself is not as easy to identify. Style is the difference between an average man in a "suit and tails" and a suave, classic dancer like Fred Astaire in suit and tails. Style methodology takes on the principles of what each human believes is comparable to or better than another. So style resides in the mind. Developing style will depend on other factors that can be controlled to a certain degree, like probing a subject without becoming off balance, promoting ideas that offer congenial answers, and avoiding the types of questions that stall or conflict with the rhythm of the conversation.

A counter-balance interview is one that attempts to put the subject off balance. Each question aims for the jugular, often making the subject fight back or become very defensive. Investigative reporting targets a topic that might be uncomfortable to the subject and the audience but is considered a worthwhile and tangible tactic to gain information that otherwise would have remained hidden.

Demeanor and attitude of the interviewer often set the mood for the interview. An approachable, highly sought-after interviewer has the power of pre-loading the scene with characteristics of his last or most famous interviews. Someone known for his style of delivery, questioning, and recognition may consider that an admirable quality. The interviewer Barbara Walters has made her career based on a tone and delivery that is often her brand. Something she's achieved over time. The subject is anticipating the type of questions that will most likely be asked. There is a tangible history between them. Sometimes that works in the subject's advantage; other times the interviewer finds himself going down a familiar road of questions or some direction he may not want to go.

A sense of style often helps determine how questions might be formed, but not necessarily the list of actual questions. Be aware of traps that place your interviewing style into a recognizable routine. Routine is boring. Find your own style and work on it. But beware that you don't minimize your integrity for flair. Your delivery and style should not overwhelm the interviewer any more than the style and reputation of your interviewee should take over completely.

Balance is in order.

~~ 2. THE BETTER INTERVIEW ~~

"The best interviews—like the best biographies—should sing the strangeness and variety of the human race."

~ Lynn Barber

What makes one interview better than the next? Much of it is subjective and found to be more ethereal than grounded to a standard. What makes a good poem? Forethought and a willingness to expose the true, emotional, raw nerve while being entertaining? Maybe. I've found that personalities who draw out the best from an interviewed person have stand-alone charisma, camera presence—in many cases—and a humanness that naturally connects you to the conditions of the interview.

It's an affirmation that you have chosen to allow a respected person into your home—by means of TV, radio, or audio device—to share a moment in time, time that would have been spent washing dishes or making dinner. If the interview goes well, you find yourself transfixed. You even want more.

Even if you are riding in your car and turn on an interview covering a topic of your interest, it has magically created what we could call an "out-of-touch experience." You know full well you are sitting and listening, but your immediate world has pushed away, leaving you totally immersed in the conversation at hand.

Did you notice that celebrity and personality come into play here? We are attracted to celebrity and bend an ear to anyone who is of higher status than we are. It's natural to want to eavesdrop, too. Radio and TV allow us the convenience of that.

With practice, anyone can become an interviewer with a following. You'll also need to get the attention of the media to place yourself as an expert. Your choices will determine whether the public likes you or ignores you.

Practice Takes Effort

Sure, practice takes effort. Ask a sports professional, a pianist, ballerina, firefighter, or top salesman. Without investing in practice sessions, or training with a recurring refresher course, you will not see any improvement as you master your interviewing skills.

The basics of speaking and listening one-on-one involve focus, eye contact, listening, breathing, and developing a question pool to engage your subject while keeping the conversation on a determined path. Even an impromptu interview is based on questions and a "prompt" directed by how your subject responds or reacts to your questions.

Let's jump right in with an example:

"Hi, Edward. It's so nice to finally meet you."

"Good to meet you, too. Sorry if I've been hard to contact."

"Oh, not at all. It's just that our schedules had never synched, but I've been following your latest project."

"You mean my movie?"

"Actually, your movie and your music video that you performed for charity last week."

As this imaginary interview continues, I would angle my

questions for more details about how the production went, when the charity became his focus, for how long, and what the charity does in general. Then angle the questions back toward him and ask how he happened to become such a prominent supporter for the charity. Wrap up with his life plans and details for next year. And finish with a plug for his new movie release.

This is a typical, celebrity-style interview where the celeb has had access to his publicist and has possibly been coached how to respond to certain questions from the public and the press.

Now, let's look at how you can practice as you gain your method of interviewing and become more comfortable in public.

It seems logical to first stand at a mirror and pretend you're interviewing your favorite celebrity. Hold a "hairbrush" microphone in your traditional interviewing stance and ask a question. Do you hold your head up? Do you slouch? Do you race through the question? Do you mumble? Does your voice squeak? Do you act *as if* you're a seasoned interviewer? Think about it.

Half the battle with speaking in public is getting the nerve to try; the other half is coming off sounding professional. Keep practicing. I'll cover many of these traits throughout the book.

Question and Answer Format

Developing the Q and A format is the standard set by most interviewers. However, don't dismiss the static format as old and boring. It's the content of the questions that truly make the difference. Make your questions compelling and built to prompt good answers with plenty of feedback. Avoid questions that offer just a "yes" or "no" answer. Those can wear you down ... not to mention your subject.

Let's look at a standard Q and A interview:

Q: "When you designed your new solar cell, did you ever think what your family and friends might say or how they might react to your sudden good fortune if it worked?"

A: "Well, no. Not really. I had to make it work correctly and efficiently under all circumstances first before I could even get a financier or any level of venture capital involved."

Q: "Was the process from creation to development to sales an arduous trail? Or was it easier than you thought?"

A: "It became everything to me. Even my family was a bit burned out by my focus on the project. I knew it would take a few years before I could claim it as a success. It was tough."

Q: "Is it the success you were pinning all your hopes and dreams on?"

A: "Definitely! My design proved to be a good moneymaker, as well as the answer to reducing solar costs for consumers."

Q: "Are you in that mansion you dreamed of?"

A: "Well, ha, not yet. I suppose the solar cells need to sell for a few years before that happens."

Q: "Things can move quickly in a new industry. So I can't imagine you sitting back, waiting for the profits to roll in. What's on your drawing board now?"

A: "You're absolutely right. I'm working with new investors on a lighting concept for industrial buildings. I can't say much right now."

Q: "I understand. You'll let us all in on your next success, right?"

A: "I sure will. Thanks."

As you work an interview, you may need to adjust how your subject responds. A new line of questions can easily lead you to more interesting topics. But beware! You are in control of the interview. You decide if the conversation is going astray or whether it's on track. And since you are in control, if your interview becomes sluggish or off track, it is your job to redirect or redesign it in mid-stride. Scary to do? Yes. Impossible? No. Quickly find a common thread from the straying topic and get the interview back on track.

For instance, a conversation might be going well, and you have not struggled too much to draw out information from your subject. Then it happens. Your subject either stops giving detailed answers, or he drifts off to other regions. Here's a simple way to get on track.

As an example:

Q: "Thanks for coming to the program. I hear that the trip to and from Bali wasn't the best experience. What happened on the runway?"

A: "Pirates. They thought every airplane was loaded with dope."

Q: "Were you able to avoid trouble?"

A: "Our crew took care of things. Logistics, and all that. I was stunned by the beauty of the jungle and all of the native people. Did you know they come right to the plane and offer fruits and flowers? They even have beautiful young ladies taking pictures of your arrival so you can send a photo home. I saw this one girl ..."

Q: "... so the pirates weren't the worst of your trouble?"

A: "Not really. I didn't even see them until we were taxiing down the runway to leave. It was a short delay. The monkeys are like all over the place. The tourists can handfeed them."

Q: "Really? According to the reports, you were held on the runway for several hours at gunpoint. Not true?"

A: "It wasn't anything to worry about. They left us alone."

Q: "Are you aware that two other airplanes in that region were shot down? How did you remain so calm?"

A: "Partly it was due to not hearing about it. Ask my producer or director. They're the ones who keep track of all that. Maybe now I can ask for a raise or hazard pay."

Q: "Sounds like you're very cool under fire."

Another faction of interviewing is falling in love with your question pool. If you've already decided to stick tenaciously to your list of selected questions, it won't be easy when cutting out or modifying your actions during the interview. Don't be so restrictive based on the pool of questions you put together. If the questions tend to fall out of order, be flexible enough to see it and adjust.

If the conversation takes a turn in a very different direction, the seasoned interviewer will see it coming and veer away, or take it and run.

The sign of a new interviewer is to become flustered when the chronological order you're relying on goes awry. The sign of a seasoned interviewer is to adjust and "duck and bob" like a pro boxer. If you're able to show flexibility, your subject will most likely appreciate your professionalism. Besides, if you're good, he and your audience will never know you're ducking and bobbing to make the interview shine.

Story Format

Everyone loves a good story. You can easily direct your questions by prompting your subject to follow your format. First, take time to understand a few traits of your subject, if possible. For instance, if the person holds any awards, sports records, or distinguished actions, you may find a parallel connection that will prompt him to share information with you. Any story angle will immediately draw in your listeners and help bond them with your interviewee. It all comes together in a story with a "good interest" topic, some defining moments, a strong or subtle climax, and a resolution that is satisfying. And, remember, even if it doesn't appear to turn out to be perfect in the end, the pathos and ultimate bond will anchor your listeners/readers to the interview content.

Let's look at a story-format interview:

In this sample, General Augustine Gallop, USMC retired, is sharing some basic information about his military career, but he's a bit stoic and uncomfortable being interviewed this time. During his extensive career, he witnessed many battle scenes and knows the military strategies it takes to control battalions. But the general is out of his comfort zone now. He needs to loosen up a bit …

Q: "When I reviewed your distinguished military career, I must admit I was overwhelmed by the extensive time you spent away from your country and family. What was it like returning to Arkansas after your last tour?"

A: "Well, as you can imagine, things changed … drastically.

Ah, my two sons had grown from toddlers to sophomore and junior in high school. I kept up with their lives as much as I could—letters, photos and videos …"

Q: "When I was in college, I felt removed and very disconnected from my family life. How did you make up for the time?"

A: "It was my wife's idea to send me a small voice recorder and a few cassette tapes. In the evenings, when the battlefield quieted down, I just began talking. I imagined I was on the telephone, talking to them."

Q: "I can picture that. It seems like a very humbling experience for you. Did you enjoy those moments?"

A: "Yes."

Q: "Did your sons respond by tape to you?"

A: "Sometimes."

Q: "As a strategist, did you recommend this form of staying connected to your officers in the field? Did it help others?"

A: "No. It was private."

Q: "So, was there a program in place to help other soldiers stay connected to their families during their military stints?"

A: "No."

As you can determine from his demeanor—his curt answers and tone of voice—he is not comfortable. He's building a wall. It's up to the interviewer to pay attention to the small signals and redirect the tone of the conversation if he wishes it to continue.

Q: "Your distinguished service medals glorify"—the general

frowns at that word and shuffles in his seat—"... rather, your career accomplishments are textbook craft. Are you aware that your documented tactics are being taught in military schools today?"

A: "I hold the high honor of being documented like Eisenhower, Patton, and Schwarzkopf. I suppose being printed in training materials is part of that process."

Q: "I understand that most military men don't like to take credit for the thousands of men who fought on the battlefield, but you were an infantryman for several tours of duty."

A: "Yes. I was planning to be a career officer, but I came into the war rather late, as most admin types will tell you. I chose to battle it out in combat first and not take the military-school direction. Once I was schooled in the field, I then applied for core training in the States."

Q: "Is that where you met Mrs. Gallop?"

A: "She found me, to be more precise. I was her stand-in at her Senior Prom. The young man who asked her had chicken pox. I was a bit older and just as awkward as a sixteen-year-old."

Q: "Did it go well at first? Was she impressed with your uniform?"

A: "Yes, it went well, and she was impressed. However, I told her she would be marrying a career man and not the uniform. I caught her a bit off guard. We married four weeks later. Then I was reassigned about four weeks after that."

Q: "She must have been a strong woman for her age in that era."

A: "She had to be … and she proved she was."

Case Study Format

A one-on-one interview is always the best scenario to work in, but there are, at times, situations where you have no control. For instance, this next case study draws from a different source. Sometimes, you'll be interviewing a person who will be delivering information third-hand. The answers to your questions may appear more generalized or created to highlight a certain event, person of interest, or product that an interviewee is proud to share with an audience.

Think of promos, perhaps a new product or a new movie, and the spokesperson, who is profoundly focused on the product, is at your fingertips. By taking any handouts or prior resources offered, you design a question pool that most commonly comes from publicist accounts, websites, direct marketing promos, marketing materials, and even old interviews. In this case, the interviewee is the conduit, the spokesperson, for the company.

Their intent is to applaud their product or services, to enrich their bottom line, while your job is to flush out the true, the realistic, the non-inflated aspects. Given a good pool of directed questions, you can make a pompous spokesperson come off as an informed- consumer reporter—a balance of questions directing toward a balance of company goals. In some cases company atmosphere and history will let the natural progression of questions follow to the enhanced treatment of the product.

This format is used quite often when a product is just being introduced to the public and the marketing department may not have the selling scenario fleshed out yet. A junior partner may be assigned to introduce the item, often without much background or time to practice. The tone of the information is delivered without much hype or character. If you're expecting it but don't see it, then you can balance what you've learned with a bit of personality to make the public interested in it.

Case studies should have as much punch and energy as a high-end marketing campaign, but they can fall short. It's up to you to find the hook and enlighten the public.

Table of Contents Format

Just like a book, the Table of Contents format leads in a regular progression and it is, by its construction, a logical trail from introduction to several topics related by interest, time, dates, development, and purpose. When completed, all topics have been resolved in an attempt to satisfy the listener. Take a moment to digest the layout of your question pool. Does each question follow progressively to your final destination? Will each question build toward the next? This format is much more structured and does not usually go off on tangents or expose a characteristic of your interviewee that you don't want to openly pursue.

Consider this written-question-pool style when submitting your questions by mail to your subject. You make contact only by mail due to your subject's request. You send some questions to be filled out and sent back as soon as possible or by a specific deadline. This is often done when the subject is not immediately available, is sick but wishes to respond, is out of the country, or even so remote that phone service is a luxury. Celebrities on shooting locations come to mind.

The toughest challenge is to temper the interviewee's long-winded and often ego-inflated responses with just enough detail to be informative but not overdone. These question pools that allow the subject to take his time and write much more than necessary can be trimmed to your satisfaction. It's up to you whether or not to return the interview for a final approval by the interviewee. Some companies demand a pre-press review; others allow "spontaneous" answers to a question pool. If you are interviewing on behalf of a publishing agency, check their protocols before you commit. Just ask in advance to make life easier for both of you.

~~ 3. THE POLICE INTERVIEW ~~

"A journalist is basically a chronicler, not an interpreter of events. Where else in society do you have the license to eavesdrop on so many different conversations as you have in journalism? Where else can you delve into the life of our times?"

~ Bill Moyers

My decision to toss police interviewing into the mix came because so many think this style is necessary. The police interview or interrogation goes back to the Inquisition. It pits the general public against the authority of the government. Although I'll admit it may be a good tool for law enforcement, its use of inner fear and retribution are not the qualities of a good interview. Part of our expectations of conducting a police interview are based on Hollywood's version of it; we need answers to fall into a 60-minute, made-for-TV, time period.

However, in the course of covering a real news story, whether it be "breaking news" or a personal profile with a tight deadline, never engage in Inquisition-style tactics. Badgering someone to tell you what you want comes close to brandishing intimidation as a weapon.

Under Duress

Protocol is the driving force of the police interview. Every department has one ... or several. Detectives will drill down to force information from the common man as well as the hardened criminal. Questions are not just offered to obtain an answer but are intended to redirect, browbeat, and coerce information from the subject who will help break a case, inform, or substantiate the reasons for someone's actions.

Most police interviews are less dramatic, rather boring, and only help establish basic facts.

Unlike TV cop shows, police interviews can last for several hours and can be manipulated by how the questions are formed and how the subject acts as he's responding. Or for that matter, how the officer is reacting to the information given. Most interview rooms record all proceedings in order to keep a running record of their suspect's progress and, eventually, to corner the person into slipping up and answering deviously to avoid the truth.

Interrogators are often specialists in extracting pertinent information from alleged witnesses and perpetrators alike. Regardless of how recalcitrant your subject may be, you'll want to avoid doing an interrogation. Your subject could easily shut down or even walk out. Not good. You'll be "red-flagged" as a self-serving, pompous, interrogating moron. Not a reputation you should desire.

A person under duress can and will say almost anything to avoid the truth, to redirect you from him, and to evade entrapment by police. Other persons under duress include victims of crime, victims of an accident or fire, and those caught in "mob" scenarios. A mob is a group of witnesses to one major incident. Each mob member will be agitated, submitting their truth in great detail, correct or not, and will swear on the Bible that what they saw was real. The oddity of the "mob syndrome" is that none of them will be reliable. Thirty pairs of eyes can see 30 different possibilities and descriptions ... useless to police investigators.

Man on the Street

I began my journalism career doing many "man on the street" interviews. Usually, a themed question was selected and proposed to random people on the street. If you have ever been approached by an interviewer, take a chance and let your voice be heard ... or recorded.

The concept is easy: write up a compelling question, take a recorder, and hit the beat. It's a good idea to take samples from every walk of life. A good cross sample of age, gender, race, and religion will give your question the wide appeal that readers like to see.

Often, the question will relate to a current topic or incident in the news. At other times it will be political in nature. People who are approached have the choice of commenting or declining. Be sure to get their first and last name and city if your protocol is to have all photos and/or recorded messages verified. Also be very careful that you attach the correct comment to the correct person. You don't want to deal with the embarrassment ... and the retraction if you misidentify or misquote someone.

About 30 percent of people you approach will refuse to take the time to answer. The question must pertain to the outcome you are striving to collect. If you come across a person who answers incoherently or makes no sense at all, thank him and move on. Believe me, you'll run into those.

Many college communication students and journalists use this format, as well as small town community newspapers. It's a process that works.

While photos are another aspect of this type of interview, it's best to talk with your subject to explain what you are doing and how important it is to get a variety of responses. Once you have the person fairly relaxed and open to the idea, then you need to ask for the photo. Most "man-on-the-street" subjects may shy away from having their photo taken, although most newspapers prefer a photo with each response. The trick to gaining a great photo and a good response is in how you approach a person you've never meet.

Some actions you might try:

- smile and openly show interest in your subject
- use a clipboard to hide the camera and/or recorder
- a clipboard in hand can break the ice on first approach
- never shove a microphone or camera in your subject's face until you've gain their trust
- introduce yourself and explain the importance of your mission
- explain that they can make a difference in their community by sharing their point-of-view
- if they refuse, be sure to acknowledge their choice as being a personal one and not anything pertaining to you
- be aware of identity theft issues and fraud, as many people avoid giving out any personal information. Honor their choices.
- when someone expresses a well-thought out opinion, tell them, and thank them for a great interview

Hard News Reporting

There are major differences in how information is gathered during a breaking news story and a typical interview. The news journalist is required to get to the scene, assess and gather enough early information to track the pertinent details, select the person or persons of authority who can give them the most accurate and critical details, follow new leads, and pose questions that will answer the basic 5-Ws of reporting:

- WHO ... is the action about; why should we care?
- WHAT ... happened that caused this incident?
- WHERE ... did it happen; does the location matter?
- WHEN ... did it occur; during a time that matters?
- WHY ... did it occur; why does this incident require reporting? Find the back story.
- and don't forget HOW ... did it happen? How will it affect the community? How much did it cost?

These basic questions are rudimentary to most cub reporters; they establish the background, tone, and immediacy to the scene and story. Interviewing techniques automatically shift to urgent basic questions and, as the story unfolds, can be directed to the most specific of interest questions taken from a witness, police, state or county officials, victim's family or co-workers, and in some cases, other news media personnel directly related to the story.

Check your local library's list of reference books for best tactics and protocol practices for on-scene reporting. The libraries are full of how-to and technical books on this subject. Your college bookstores also house the current list of journalism textbooks for raw recruits.

Since my focus is on interviewing skills for common uses, I won't try to fill the shoes of an industry that has literally written the book on interviewing. Journalism is a well-defined profession and one that needs to be studied for much longer that a few hundred pages.

For general news gatherers, hard news reporting is typically different because the interviewer doesn't have the time to develop a question pool, has limited resources to tap into, avoids any personality profiling, and keeps high focus on gathering those hard facts. The reporter must select only the facts that will fill the 5-Ws and 1-H by deleting minor details that may diffuse the immediacy of the current event.

Early on, journalism students learn the "Pyramid" form of writing hard news in which the top details rise to the lead paragraph, and all other details fall into diminishing positions. This design allows the editing department to trim away at the bottom of the story to fit the space without deleting pertinent details.

If the story is written correctly, all but the first, lead paragraph can be removed, leaving the story, although sparse, adequate to the reader. This technique can be used in any writing format. It keeps your thoughts focused and trains your brain to weed out extraneous fluff and description.

The feature story in news reporting fills that gap between hard news and editorials. A feature story is more timely; it is often a hard news story that may need fleshing out. To the general audience, it can answer many more questions—days or even weeks later—regarding the topic that first appeared as a hard news item. For the writer it requires much more research and planning, allows the personality of the focused subject to come through, and gives a softer edge to the tone of the original news story.

Let's take a closer look:

An elderly woman is taken into custody over a dispute about a tree. The huge sycamore tree will be chopped down because it poses a threat to the community. It's old and possibly diseased, and the city fears it will fall down and injure or kill someone.

The old woman stands fast and will not be swayed. She won't even tell the reporters why she is adamantly opposed. She doesn't trust anyone. The police lose their patience with her, and she's driven away in a police cruiser.

The next day an injunction is served on the city to stop and desist any killing, removing, burning, or disfiguring of the sycamore.

A news reporter who covered the first story is now interested in finding the reasons why an elderly, unassuming woman would place herself in the way of the authorities. After being asked by his news editor to follow up on the story, he researches what he can find, then talks to a few of her neighbors, who describe her as sweet and never known to cause trouble, although she seems a bit senile.

The reporter makes an appointment to interview the woman, although she is apprehensive. He tells her she can now tell her side of the story. They sit in her garden and he records her on his personal recorder while taking some written notes to capture the tone and style of her speech.

She states her case: She is upset that they would cut down a perfectly good tree. She's been on her property for over 55 years, raised her family here, and buried her husband recently at the cemetery down the street. The tree should be able to live its life without being uprooted.

An hour later the reporter has gathered the targeted answers he was aiming for. The woman will soon be selling her home. Her family is forcing her into a residential care facility due to her declining health. She feels that the tree is paralleling her life to some degree. Seeing them ready to "hack it down" only strengthens her own fear. She fears people are too much in a hurry to get rid of old things. Then she reveals the deeper connection. Her husband has died and she wants to cling to his memory as long as she can. Her memory is fading yet she always remembers the time he carved his name in the old sycamore tree.

After the interview, the feature story was highlighted on page one, showing the woman, her home from the curbside view, and the carved memories in the bark of the old tree. The city hired a horticulturist to inspect the tree to see if it was worth saving. Their findings allowed the tree to stay for a few more years. It was eventually taken down, but only after the old woman lost her battle to ailing health.

In a perfect world, the reporter would have done a follow-up feature on the demise of the tree and the woman who stood strong for each other.

Without an in-depth interview, we would never have known the full background of the story, the pathos of the lives the tree represented, its ultimate outcome, and the feelings expressed through the printed word, all of which effected much more than the neighborhood. It makes for a good story.

Journalistic writing can be broken down into many categories, based on the technique of discovery, depth of research, topic, and demographics. The single thread that ties them together throughout each process is the interview.

~~ 4. WHY SOME INTERVIEWS SHINE ~~

"As life runs on, the road grows strange with faces new—and near the end. The milestones into headstones change, 'Neath every one, a friend."

~ James Russell Lowell

Ask anyone in the communications and advertising industries and you'll find that a story always sells; it's a given. People love insider information, those emotional connections with a lip-smacking story that stimulates and entertains. Ever since native man exchanged folklore and family history with his tribesmen, storytelling has captured the vision and the tone of his culture. Things haven't changed.

However, nothing is really different in its content; it's the delivery. The written word preserves. The narrated story lives on.

Imagine reading the story of how your close ancestors packed up and moved to a new state. They had no idea what was ahead, but they embraced the adventure because it wasn't where they once were. Each relative in the move west collected their own memories. In later years they would tell the story repeatedly. Most details became the standard they shared in the retelling of it.

Telling a "yarn" is not quite the same. Just because Uncle Wilbur is good at fabrication doesn't mean he can separate the truth from the sublime. He may be able to, but it's a clear fact that he may not want to. That's where legends come from.

Sitting around a campfire several generations later, the stories of granddad's covered-wagon ride through Indian-infested prairies conjures up pictures, scents, and sounds of the ordeal. You'll recall the verbal stories with messages and morals, battles and great warriors, crop failures, births and deaths, and major migrations.

If told enough times, it becomes indelible. Just ask a grandchild to retell one of their grandparents' stories. How boring and dry it would be to read only the bare facts: they packed up, drove out across the prairies, and settled in the West. No color, no connection, no life breathed into the telling of it. All the details might be present, but when given in a narrative story format, all the adventure manifests once again.

Stories Sell

When choosing how to develop an idea, consider its format. How energizing it could be, for instance, to study biology with an instructor who draws you into the realm of flora and fauna with an enticing story. Let him tell you how he flew to South Africa on safari, where he hunted the endangered but poisonous "something-or-other" lizard. I would be fighting for a front row seat if my teacher had enticed me with a good story. Children think teachers are boring. Coeds think professors are uptight. Fortunately, I had a great U.S. History professor in college who enticed us with interesting stories. Thank you, Mr. Varty.

You can learn all there is to know about that lizard in a textbook. But you'll never forget the colorful details of how the lizard was caught, photographed, analyzed, and released then written about for the textbook.

Remember that the level of engagement and how it's presented and emotionally supported become the rewards of a good story.

So when it comes to an interview, the subject must be prompted to share their experiences in a story format, incurring those same familiar feelings that Storytime invokes.

The best way to practice is to interview a close family member who knows your family history. If you select a grandmother or favorite older aunt, ask her questions that will prompt a series of reminiscences. Tell her that memories in story form will help her put her thoughts into special groupings such as birthdays, major incidents related to how the family coped, deaths, and other milestones.

If you have access to an upper-management, professional, business owner or president, ask a series of questions that prompt his or her climb up the ladder. Be sure to follow with a continuing question that builds on the previous one.

Let's Look at a Story Format Question Pool:

In this sample, let's assume we are interviewing Grandma Lois from Minnesota. She is in her late 80s and has lived most of her life in her home state.

Q: "It's been awhile since we talked, but I hear that you just moved into a retirement home. How are things going?"

A: Her answer might be bitter, well-thought out, or timid, depending on her experiences there.

Q: "Can you explain what differences you like about your new home?"

A: After she points out, let's say, three differences, lead her to elaborate on one that you choose. Give her time to think. If she is prompted by her own memories of Minnesota as she considers your question, allow her to lead.

Q: "How were able to stay single in Minnesota for so long after your husband's death. Were you ever scared?"

A: Her answer might surprise you. A surprise is a gift to follow. Base your questions now on the tangents that you hear, and express interest in her situation.

Q: You know the family members, so ask about one member who no one really talks about.

A: Again, her answers might surprise you.

Follow that elusive train of thought, but keep your ears open for interesting tangents. It's okay to have quiet moments while thinking of those memories, but if your subject takes too long or becomes distant, it's up to you to pull her back onto the conversation track. Family photo albums are a great starting point if you feel your conversation needs a punch of energy.

With practice you can move up to friends, their parents, a co-worker, a church elder, or anyone you know but may not know well. Part of the reward of a good interview is drawing out the nuggets and defining personality traits that are meaningful, entertaining, and fulfilling.

Today, with the instant connections the Internet hands us, you can easily conduct a search for historical interviews. Dick Cavett and David Frost are two internationally known interviewers who enjoyed a major following in the '70s. TV shows based on celebrity entertainment and interviews can be located by searching "Dick Cavett Shows" and "Interviews with David Frost." There is also the recent movie, "Frost/Nixon," which is based on dramatic interviews with British journalist Sir David Frost and former president Richard Nixon. Also check out the gems that celebrity interviewers have conducted. Among them are: Oprah Winfrey, Barbara Walters, Larry King, entertainment influences by "Entertainment Tonight," and written interviews in

People Magazine and *Playboy*. Yes, even *Playboy* has exemplified some outstanding interviews over the years.

Within the structure of the interview, the story that tells more details, that exemplifies the ethics and tone of the story, and the regional influxes of how the story is shared all infuse a high quality of history. It's the connectedness that makes a story shine. Remember that we are trying to pull information from someone who may not be a great communicator but who, with our ultimate goal at hand, must give up some nuggets of information that will keep our viewers or readers mesmerized.

Also be aware that when interviewing a professional person of a large corporation, for instance, the same rules really do apply. You can extract details that will exemplify the ethics and tone of the workplace or corporate atmosphere, highlight the regional influxes of how the workplace is reflected in the corporation, and chronicle key events of company history that can create connectedness for your viewer. Your goal is to weave a good story into your interview, whether in written form or taped, verbal conversation that will be broadcast later.

Some interviews won't go as smoothly as others. Your developing expertise and expanding ability to suggest and manipulate the ebb and flow of the interview will improve with practice. Ask anyone in the corporate world who has been interviewed for a syndicated TV program, and you'll see them roll their eyes, fidget, and even break into a sweat. Being grilled and filmed is not the easiest thing to survive. Make the effort to leave your subject with the feeling that the interview went well, and he'll let you and your colleagues return. However, as with the corporate atmosphere and the title, comes the requirement of being a "Subject Matter Expert" or SME. Someone is bound to catch you in an elevator—so be ready.

From another perspective, if you wish to engage your audience with a tantalizing tale and fulfilling interview, you'll need to create the environment for a good story. Everyone loves a good story, and as the interviewer, it's up to you to capture it.

Storytelling is basic and embedded in our genes somewhere back in Neanderthal times. Every culture and every age bracket can easily associate with a story that offers information that is easily digestible, savory, and fulfilling. It's edible education served on an antique silver platter. Even if they are different language groups, their story still captures and entertains.

To make my point more concise, I've asked Daphne Gray-Grant, a writing and editing consultant, to step in with a few strategic reasons why storytelling is used in fiction and non-fiction roles. It's compelling information, and I'm glad she's sharing her expertise for your benefit.

Seven Darn Good Reasons Why You Should Tell Me a Story
(published with permission)

A group of judges is gathered in court. But instead of looking grand and imperial in their robes, they appear to be naked. And puzzlingly, they are arrayed, under blankets, in a selection of beds spread out behind the bench.

No, let me reassure you this didn't happen in real life. It's simply a cartoon from the *New Yorker*. A lone lawyer stands at a microphone in front of the justices, receiving instructions. The caption? "O.K., counselor, we heard your argument. Now tell us a story. Yes, please, please. Tell us a story."

Most parents of three-year-olds can probably relate to this cartoon. But so should you! Telling stories—and telling them well—is probably the single most important job facing any writer. And guess what? Stories aren't just for novelists. They're for everyone from the CEO to his or her most junior communications staffer.

Here are seven reasons why you should work hard at telling more stories in your non-fiction writing:

1)   Stories have a natural rhythm. Tell a story and you'll automatically start with the most interesting material. At the same time, you'll give details exactly where they belong and you'll end by reinforcing the key point you want to make. This kind of structure gives you a big, paint-by-numbers approach to your work. It helps make writing easier and less painful.

2)   Stories humanize the realities of the business world. Have you ever sat through speeches and started to drift off into ZZZZZ-land as the speakers rambled on about statistics or core values? And yet, didn't you snap to attention when they suddenly told you a story about something that happened in the office or, better yet, a story about their own, non-work lives? We're all hardwired to love stories. Growing up and getting a serious job doesn't change that one iota.

3)   Stories carry a sense of momentum; they have their own natural tension. The middle of a good story leaves the reader wondering, "Yeah, and what happened *next?*" As a writer, isn't that *exactly* what you want—readers desperate for your next sentence?

4)   Stories are sticky or, in other words, memorable. More than 16 years ago—I know the timeframe because it was before my children were born—I heard a radio interview with career coach Barbara Sher, author of *I Could Do Anything If I Only Knew What it Was.* This woman is a masterful speaker, and I'll never forget her

story about a cab driver who wanted to become a cake baker. She advised the driver to launch her career by baking "surprise" and anonymous cakes for major public events. Turns out the woman succeeded by having one of her cakes cause a big—and positive—sensation at an event in Chicago. While I wouldn't advise that approach now, post 9/11, I highly recommend telling memorable stories. That I remembered this cake anecdote for 16 years should be a testament to the theory.

5) Stories force you to use concrete language. People get into writing trouble when they start using too many abstract words. You know what I mean—Superman's motto of "truth, justice, and the American Way" is a great example of abstract language. Instead, better writers talk about things you can touch, taste, smell, and hear—concrete words. Such language helps create visual images in the readers' minds. If I say the word "association," do you get a clear visual image? Probably not! But if I say, desk, or flower, or dog, your mind's eye likely creates a picture. Add even a simple verb, such as, "sits," "smells" or "barks," and the picture is clearer. Stories will keep you in the world of the concrete. Strong visual images = good writing.

6) Stories will help make your writing more believable. I don't know about you, but I've always been astonished by the number of movies and TV shows that make a big deal about being based on *true* stories. (Frankly, I always think good fiction is more amazing!) But there's something in the human psyche that loves the concept of being true to life. Tell your own stories, and you'll be satisfying a basic human need.

7) Stories allow people to persuade *themselves* of

the point you're trying to make. You then simply become the person who is presenting the evidence. And the better your stories, the more persuasive you will be.

NOTE: Daphne Gray-Grant is a writing and editing coach and the author of the popular book *8½ Steps to Writing Faster, Better,* available on her website *http://www.publicationcoach.com/*

Remember, you want an interview that tells a good story and a story that sells a good memory.

When Your Subject Works the Room

Sometimes, you'll come across a subject who is used to being interviewed. Usually a celebrity, he's sharp, well liked, a natural speaker, comfortable, and easy to talk to. Sometimes he is so comfortable that he takes over the interview and begins working the room like a politician stumping for votes. A charmer, he knows how a live interview works. You'll have to be on top of your game to match his. You'll need to balance his likeability to the audience with your need to cover certain questions.

Once you gain a direction in your question pool, try to keep your subject focused. Let the interview work naturally, but as soon as you notice him gaining his own momentum, try to redirect him back to your line of questioning. Mimic a phrase he has used and incorporate it into the interview in your attempt to redirect.

Let's look at a specific redirect phrase to get him back to your question pool about his current movie, *Seaworthy*.

In this sample, your celebrity subject is speaking about his female co-star in *Two Tanks* but then mentions three other supporting actors. You don't wish to overload the focus of your interview with too many other personalities or films, so you select a phrase he has used to re-emphasize your position:

"After working with Sally, it was a pleasure to find my outdoor scenes with Todd, Jane, and Alexis so easy to do. I've got two more films coming up with Jane and then Todd."

"Do you find that your outdoor scenes are easier to master because of friendships you've developed with Hugh and Jay on the ocean in *Seaworthy* and now with *Two Tanks*?

By redirecting his phrase into your question, you have easily brought him back to the focus of your questions. It's your job to keep him there and on track. This tactic can work for a corporate interview as well.

There's a fine line between struggling to keep control without looking like you're struggling and allowing the subject to entertain without openly walking away with your audience. You need to develop a fine ear for catch phrases and colorful description that prompts a new question just in case your interviewee veers off.

Your ability to learn how to temper your focus with his, however, will make your interview engaging but not constricted, informative but not stalled, and colorful yet confidently controlled. Sometimes, the engaging person working the room is harder to control than a shy, demure personality.

The Confident Subject

I feel the best interview is one held with a confident and comfortable subject. He's capable of delivering a colorful story without taking full control, knows what the listeners like, avoids boredom, enjoys being interviewed to share his knowledge, and relies on you to monitor his answers so you get the best out of him.

Those kinds of interviews favor perfection—pure gems.

For many years in the 1970s, "The Dick Cavett Show" was considered a high-quality, interview-format television program that brought celebrities, notable writers and playwrights, famous scientists, and emerging names in the film industry to light. It was often entertaining because Cavett was able to release the average man from within. His questions aimed directly but were gauged to offer the subject a choice of a solid answer instead of a wavering "yes" or "no." The subject often determined his style, yet Cavett always had an impish naiveté in his smile, his eyes, and his demeanor. He appeared to be like the little boy who had raced to the circus before sunrise and raised the edge of the tent to steal a glimpse of the elephant. His audiences compared him to Robert Redford, with a knack for prying stimulating and often amusing stories out of every person he interviewed.

If you get a chance to look up old episodes of the show on the Internet, you'll see Cavett's delivery and use of phrasing to direct his interviews.

The confident subject knows that being interviewed is part of the marketing of his business, his services, or himself. However you look at it, we all are marketing ourselves when it comes to public awareness and getting "face time" in the public eye.

A marketing-savvy person learns how to control his answers in order to bend your questions to his fulfillment. So as you interview him and sense that his answers are neatly twisting back to his personal agenda, you have a choice to either allow him to lead for a while, thereby taking full advantage of his wealth of information you won't need to pry from him later, or attempt to redirect him from sounding like a canned, announcement-heavy, brand advocate.

You can see where this is leading. No one wants a tug-a-war of personalities vs. control tactics, especially on television, radio, or live Internet feed. In other words, an interview with a well-rehearsed spokesperson, who knows his business well and loves to manipulate the interview to focus on his specifics, marks itself as a tough one.

Face it, if your subject is comprised of a "larger-than-life" ego, fed by his expertise-laden and very driven goal of getting his message across while flashing an "A Personality" smile, then you're probably in for a rough ride. (See my previous chapter.) However, if your subject shows a versatile, flexible, professional style with a knack for hedging his personal directives as he senses the tone of the questions, then you'll have a great interview. You can sit back and enjoy the ride.

Luckily, most interviews fall in the middle. You'll need to find a way for him to loosen up, diverge from his marketing script, and follow your line of questions. Can it be done? Sure. But how is he thinking? How can you understand what his goals are, or how he wishes to represent himself and his company, for instance, when he's never been interviewed before? Has he been coached? Is he comfortable as a subject? Will he make his mom proud?

One of the best ways to get inside the head of your subject is to reverse roles.

Take on the persona of your somewhat nervous but willing subject. You can learn a lot and defuse more than nerves by understanding him. What makes him become nervous? Has he previously been interviewed? If you read in him that he won't do well in front of a camera, for instance, can you speak to him off stage? Can you bolster his confidence? Can you get him ready for your interview? By walking a half-mile in his shoes or role-playing, you'll gain a better insight as to how you can select questions for his interview. Just stop short of holding his hand.

The old adage, "Let him walk a mile in my shoes," is appropriate here. So, to prepare for role-reversals, I've asked another colleague to help.

Now let's take a look at a short excerpt from Paul Lima's information-packed strategy paper, "How To Prepare For Interviews."

> To prepare for interviews, think about the most pertinent information you want to convey. Write out potential questions and your answers. Keep your answers short and focused—about 20 to 45 seconds per answer. Supplement answers with anecdotes about your products, services, or customers that help demonstrate what you want to say. If possible, get permission to "drop the name" of an established customer that has benefited by working with you.
>
> As you answer questions, judiciously repeat key messages for emphasis, but make sure you also answer the questions so you don't sound like you are in "spin" mode—like a politician during an election campaign (or at any time, for that matter).
>
> This might sound simple to do; however, unless you prepare, you might forget to convey information you want to express, you might convey the wrong information, or you might convey information that circumstances dictate should be held back until you are authorized to release it. On the other hand, if you are prepared, you will be able to articulately reply to the interview questions.

NOTE: Paul Lima is a freelance writer and media interview trainer. Visit him online at www.paullima.com. Request a free "How to Prepare for Interviews" report by emailing writer@paullima.com.

You must be able to recognize that your interviewee has the need to field questions with a focus, has most-likely prepped and practiced so he comes across more comfortable in his role, and has fleshed out his personal answers with information that will ultimately put a spin on his delivery. He may be aware that he needs to keep a professional air to both his side and your side of the interchange. Let's just hope he remembers to smile.

Now that you know this, help him reach his best personal performance by making him comfortable and letting him give a few prepped answers. But also dig deeper. Pull information from him, define his personality, let him be real. Allow the reader/listener/viewer to be satisfied. Without your audience, you have nothing more than a good conversation. Always keep your audience in mind.

The Exclusive Interview

One of the highlights of most well-known interviewers is the long-awaited or highly-sensitive exclusive interview. These, of course, are coveted by networks to get ratings, by magazines to get readers, and even by interviewers to get and build on a reputation.

Sometimes, the exclusive may take years to set up, due to the hermit-like style of the subject or because of the notoriety of the topic and celebrity. Exclusives, while considered often of national prominence, can be of local or regional status as well.

Perhaps the largest benefactor of a museum has continually refused to speak to the media, but an up-coming benefit has the potential to draw him out into the public eye. The public carries much weight. They want to know. Well, he is reclusive, and that makes him exclusive. Your ability to persuade him to speak with you hinges on preparation, timing, knowing some insights, and luck.

Make this your chance to show how you can interview, while remaining respectful, as curious as your readers/viewers, and totally comfortable with your subject and the topic. I should add a disclaimer here: *all the prep and legwork in the world will not guarantee success in being granted an interview, but certain methods will help you.*

Here's a list of preparation ideas to help you gain the information you'll need:

- Check the library for printed news items
- Review old interviews
- Talk to family, if possible
- Check the Internet
- Cross-references
- Talk to friends and past colleagues
- Keep it fresh
- Find a "Hook"
- Develop a pool of questions
- Offer your questions in advance

Although not all journalists or writers agree on this practice, offering your questions in advance can often help break down barriers. A list of questions gives the interviewee time to research specific answers, thus avoiding embarrassing voids in the conversation or a subject who says, "I can't comment on that." Most journalists refuse to hand out their question pool due to two reasons: they are professional and don't wish to be directed by anyone; and they want fresh and immediate answers, nothing canned.

When I interview small businesspersons, I will often ask them if they have ever been interviewed before. If they say no, I offer a list of questions in advance but also tell them that, during the interview, I have the freedom to ask other questions as they come up. This gives the person a base to work from and the forewarning of possible other questions that he might not be prepared for. The mix usually works well. The interviewee is more relaxed.

If your exclusive is a current event, then be sure to study the latest news, and research the topic extensively on your own. Know everything you can about the pros and cons and how your readers will interpret the significance of this interview event.

Let's consider an on-camera interview of a notable-but-reclusive celebrity:

Opt for a comfortable environment by providing water and a box of tissues nearby. Consider camera angles and their placement when working with a camera crew. If a production assistant makes suggestions on camera angles, then let him do his job. Don't be a Stephen Spielberg by directing, producing, and controlling every aspect yourself. You may find yourself back in that same studio with a different interviewee but with the same studio staff grumbling in the wings.

You may also find that your subject will only talk to you at his home. Your subject may prefer to control his environment based on health issues or just personal preferences. Find out what you can do to make him comfortable. Then find out how to make the camera crew comfortable. It's up to them to make you look good. There's no guarantee that you can even have cameras around, so plan on a taped interview only. But take copious notes.

Work on your delivery, your lead-ins, and your transition phrases. If others practice doing a good interview for you, then by all means, show them how ready you are.

Things to avoid: stammering, picking at your face or nose,

laughing too hard, saying "uh" or "um" too much, allowing your eyes to be distracted from your subject, losing focus, losing your place, using distracting notes on your lap, licking your lips too often, and smiling like a goon …

Okay, so that last one I tossed in after watching an afternoon regional interview show where the emcee was interviewing someone while exhibiting a wide, flashy smile that was frozen to his face throughout the entire show.

Cue cards and teleprompters are tools you should become comfortable with. Stop at a studio and ask for a tour. Ask to talk to the assistant producer of regional programming to see how a show goes together. Sometimes, they'll help you; sometimes, they won't. It won't hurt to ask. If you find resistance, then send a letter to the station manager and ask for some time to become familiar with the studio. Stand on the stage and actually look at the prompters and cameras. This may be the environment you'll be working in. Make this the time that defines you from the other interviewers out there. Your goal is to avoid freezing up or sweating more than the person you're interviewing. Please.

Once the interview is complete, be sure to offer a copy to your subject, send a "thank you" card, a small gift, or both, and even a request for a follow-up later in the year. Can't hurt to ask.

Sometimes, they will ask to see the interview before it's published or aired. They want to edit your product. Politely say no. You own the interview; they allowed you to interview them. A complimentary copy afterward is fine, but avoid allowing anyone to control the product and control the output. That's what courts are for.

If you are the ethical professional that you represented to them and you've completed your job, then there is no good reason for them to want to edit your work. Some public-relations-agency reps may demand a preview. You're treading on thin ice here.

First, consider the tone of the interview. Were you confrontational and/or did you sensationalize the content, or do you believe you handled the interview with finesse?

Next, consider if the agency representing your subject has a reputation for lawsuits and whether you want to stand firm against them. Better have a lawyer in the wings.

Then, check the terms of the studio, the clients you may be working for, or the corporation you represent, if any other than yourself, to see how you should handle the request. Most journalists will admit that standing firm, with their newspaper supporting the journalist's right to control the information, is a scary situation to be in. With the privilege of First Amendment Rights, lawsuits can happen.

If you are an independent writing contractor just starting out, talk to a media lawyer. You may need to consider that a preview of your work is part of the business. If you allow it, make a proposal in writing that none of the content will be changed until a meeting is held. A preview is allowing all parties to assess the product without discrimination, warrant of prosecution, or demand to change the product. If they don't like what they see, negotiate. Perhaps a section can be deleted. But if the whole product becomes contentious, bow out and consult an attorney. If they don't like what they see, they'll be doing the same.

Libel lawsuits have always been in the news. Standing firm as a writing consultant is not quite the same as standing firm with a newspaper conglomerate and a bank of lawyers bolstering your confidence.

I highly advise that you consult a libel lawyer who deals with printed media. It will save you time and humiliation if your project fails in the eye of the interviewee. There have been times when the need for a pre-consultation helps to pave the way for the interview. I personally haven't run into that, but it can happen. If you feel you can accept your subject and his PR man editing your work, then you can. It's just not considered a typical working relationship.

Many pitfalls cover the paths to freelance interviewing. However, if you are aware and take precautions, most of your subjects will work with you and not against you. Use the tools at your disposal, record your conversations, and keep all signed contracts in a safe place. You never know when you may need them.

~~ 5. EVERYONE HAS A STORY TO SHARE ~~

*"Either write something worth reading
or do something worth writing."*

~ Benjamin Franklin

I have always been mesmerized by the concept that every one of us has a story to tell. The milkman who delivered to the famous screen stars long before the home delivery service faded, or the early inventor of some item that we now take for granted.

What is also fascinating is that people who think they should write a book don't; neighbors who think you should write a book about your colorful life experiences leave you wondering if you can. And those who *think* they never did anything outstanding or heroic to be considered in a book are often the most worthy.

The Ghostwriter

Many of the books that focus on an autobiography or non-fictional treatment are written by ghostwriters. It's not that the book is fake, it's that a professional writer was hired to help make the book a readable product. Not everyone can write. If an agent thinks his celebrity client needs a book, then the odds are that a ghostwriter will be interviewed to see if he is compatible to do the job.

Not all writers are ghostwriters or have the ability to work in the background while the celebrity gets the credit. Finding the right ghostwriter can make the difference between the success and failure of the product and whether the celebrity and agent are satisfied with the process.

If you are ever offered the chance to ghostwrite, by all means take the offer and try your hand at it. You may need to tuck your ego in your pocket, but the experience will make you a better writer, reader, and interviewer. The process is often arduous, pitting the subject against his agent, the public, a deadline, and you. On the brighter side, a good working relationship can easily enhance the entire project, eventually making it a good read. It is a significant process in which you, as the writer, become the eyes and ears of your client, reading your client's mannerisms and interviewing for not only topics, timelines, and temperament, but also for regional dialect, formation of ideas and thoughts, and personality.

If you can't be with him during the interviews, make sure you can tape record the sessions so you capture his tone and dialect. During the creative phase, send several chapters to be checked by the client, if possible. Don't rely on the client's agent to okay the work for him. It's also important to stick to a tight deadline for work approval so the client and the finished product avoid becoming lost in the daily ups and downs of a busy celebrity. Relying on the agent to run interference for you may not be a good tactic. Always ask for a direct, private line to the client, but keep the agent in the loop. You don't want a project to get flushed down the toilet based on someone's ego getting bruised.

The process of ghostwriting is no different than a standard book. Well, yes, it is. You are not the creator; your client is. You'll need to be up on your game for interviewing and collecting the data for the book. Some clients will be proactive, asking for updates as you work and offering content, stories, photos, and direction. The ease of working with a client is based on how well you get along with someone "looking over your shoulder," making changes, making suggestions, or being a nuisance. And yet, you may find a client who allows you to do your thing without interference until the product is in first draft.

I was a ghostwriter for an Italian-American WWII veteran who lived a colorful and dangerous life here and abroad. His escapades drew us into a world filled with narrow escapes, ironic near misses, and health problems only an alley cat with an excess of lives could survive. His ability to write was restricted by his lack of schooling but his storytelling captured the edginess of his days, his working years, and his eight decades; each page, scrawled in pen, nearly illegible. We worked through the pages and gradually formed a chronological storyboard and table of contents.

His wife read the first draft and approved. He was humbled by the thought that he could write a book that meant so much to him and his extended family. He chose to self-publish through a vanity press. His book is still available at www.amazon.com as of this writing: *Born to Survive, Will to Live* by Anthony G. Pasqualetti, 2005, ISBN: 1-4208-4602-7 (sc).

From an interviewing perspective, you have several choices to capture pertinent information. Tape the sessions so nothing will be lost, take copious notes to help you define how the sessions came across, or both. Be diligent in your note taking. You may never get a second chance. Is your client on a melancholy trail through very old, cloudy memories? Then show that in the tone of the session. Does she long for the days when she was a notable person? Then allow for that tone without making it sound as if she was a has-been at age 21. A good autobiography tells a tale but ultimately wraps you in the storyteller's experience, molds your perspective, and hands you the sounds and senses of that time.

The gift of interviewing and writing the outcome changes how the time elements have mellowed your client. In most cases the client is sharing behind-the-scenes stories that may affect numerous people. Concern yourself with tapping the sources of the stories and how they may have affected those at that time. How did people react? What were the headlines of the times that might have swayed their opinions? An amount of background research is part of the overall package. Don't take short cuts. The chapters you create to define the collection of memories will help keep the data moving forward.

As you go through the first and second drafts, help your client weed out the extraneous parts. Tighten it up and try to keep the finished book under 300 pages. If the book needs fleshing out in areas, you can offer to call on his friends or colleagues. Talk to others who, after knowing your client, may have changed their lives because of him. Is he an influential man but too modest to tout his own accomplishments? Maybe you have some investigating of your own to do. Fill out the details that colleagues can offer. But always remember to honor your client's life and persona. Never become an antagonist. If a friend's story conflicts with your client's, tell your client's story. It's his story and you are just the chronicler.

Some book contracts allow the ghostwriter to claim credit in the title pages, the acknowledgments, or even on the cover. Some would rather not let the public know that a ghostwriter wrote the book. Sharing credits is not always an equitable trade. Your name is in lights, in glow sticks, in candles, or under a basket. In any case, a ghostwritten book is owned by the client. So get over it.

Be sure to enjoy the ride. Express your interest and offer ideas how to enhance each anecdote. Smile and have fun. This experience may go on for a while. Don't let the job become tedious for you or for your client. First drafts can take as long as three to six months, even longer. You listen, compile, weed through, add photos, and decide on the length and focus of the book, while all the time using your interviewing skills to maintain a professional quality.

Learn as much as you can about your subject. You'll come on board aware of old rivals, bad marriages, bad choices, influences, good times and lost loves. However, rein in your "gossip rag" genes, and opt for quality stories. Focus on your outline or table of contents. It's a balancing act. Your client will respect you for that.

Once the book is complete, second and third drafts become final, and you've chosen the photos and written the captions, let the book rest for a week. Come back to it with fresh eyes.

Select a few of your client's friends who may wish to read the book prior to publishing. Get some feedback. Ask for reviews from colleagues that you can add to the back cover. Let them "sell" your book. Testimonials flavor the cover and entice others to read. Be sociable and open to new clients. Be sure to get client referrals for other books in the future.

You just never know when the next interview or book will appear.

Now, as they say, the hard part begins. Marketing your finished book as a co-author or ghostwriter may entitle you to be interviewed. Depending on how your written contract with the client has been drafted, you may have royalty rights, be asked to help market the book, or other options.

Check with the experts. Bookshelves are overloaded with experts' advice. Check out a few and use them as guides to market your new product. Take the advice of the pros: cover your legal sanctions, as well as the corporate ones. Prior to signing any contract, ask questions of the publisher to see how they might approach marketing. Your client will have the last word, but be sure you are not left out of the negotiations.

Be flexible on this. Your ability to interview goes both ways. If allowed, make the marketing your springboard to other prospects who might desire your services. The more you can help in the selling process, if you wish, the more you'll be receiving in compensation for your time beyond the flat rate of writing the book.

The Expert

In some situations you'll be asked to work directly with an expert. Experts don't always know how to write. Sure, they know their field of expertise, but they usually are aware that, to get their knowledge out into the public, they'll need a writer—and that entails a thorough interview.

Some thesis-heavy papers are first written by SMEs—Subject Matter Experts—then transformed into scientific papers and then into layman's terminology for general readership.

Interviewing a technology expert can be tasking and frustrating. You'll need to be up on your game. Their jargon is often something you've never heard; they know whereof they speak. You can ask a lot of questions, take good notes, or be coached by your own SME who will help you work through the rough draft after the initial interview. Tape these conversations, just to be on the safe side. If the jargon is throwing off your game, then be sure to hire someone you can partner with who is immersed in their industry.

If your client demands more than you can offer, bow out and thank him for the chance to be considered. It won't do you any good to suffer through a bad choice in clients, subject, or arrangement.

If you do take on the assignment, be sure to have your client or his associate re-read all of your text to verify that it is correct and that specific jargon is used to maintain the level of readership and quality you both expect. Writing for an expert is almost like writing a reference book. The exacting science of an expert forces all parties to perform at ultimate quantified levels.

This is the time you don't sweat over the expert's review; you accept it with humility.

The Wannabe

The person who wishes to be held in high esteem can often be the interview from hell. A personality quirk makes them think that everything they say must be held in strictest confidence and raised to the highest level of authority. Sometimes you won't be able to distinguish a "wannabe" from an "SME" on first meeting. They have a knack of reeling you in for their own motives. Once you have started the interview process, something will make you feel that not everything you see is on the up-and-up. Wannabes have the ability to sponge up everyone else's knowledge and spin it with their own signature before sharing it with you or the world.

Beware of wannabes. They can sap your time, your space, and your reputation. Even though you may wish to help them, they are on a mission to look better at your expense. Their stories have no depth; their figures are sketchy; and their timeline is often skewed. It's like reading a Western paperback novel and finding significant flaws in historic details and anachronisms such as pistols that weren't made when the story takes place.

The wannabe is an unpleasant fact of life. They are everywhere, so be cautious.

The Success Story

In your adventures as an interviewer, you'll find the occasional need to write for magazines or newspapers that specialize in "personality pieces." These are often spotlights on a financial whiz, a new business venture, an invention, a partnership, or a "special interest" story with a family facing a crisis.

Everyone loves a good success story. As an interviewer, your job is to pull the nuggets from the stream. How did they do what everyone had tried before? What made them achieve their success? What were the stumbling blocks? How did they cope?

If the story hinges on one lead person of a company or organization, make him the spokesperson for the group. If there is a "stand out" personality, focus on him. If there's an unassuming person forced to take on a larger role, then bring him to the forefront. A good success story is made of personalities that go the distance. Find one and let him pull you through his tribulations until you get the quality-rich story that folks love to read.

As an example: There were two men who had open-heart surgeries on the same day, same hospital, same time, and same blood type. They married in different towns, lived different lives under different circumstances, yet both retired in nearly the same week in the very same town. They never knew each other until after surgery, when they shared the same room. Now that's a story worth telling.

If your subject seems very shy and doesn't understand what all the attention is about, you may need to explain that while he may not see his accomplishment as significant, his neighbors and community see it as an astounding feat carried out by an unassuming man. This counterpoint is often the catalyst that draws readers.

The Failure Story

While not the most common theme, the failure story entrances readers due to its pathos its attempts beyond belief, or its near success that turns readers into cliffhanger junkies. The need to know, even if it's not a good outcome, is often enough.

Often, failure stories leave readers feeling unfulfilled and depressed, so use a feel-good spin to wrap it up. This tactic helps readers understand that not all stories have a perfect ending, but there are circumstances where a lesser benefit is good enough.

A failure story may focus on the guy striving to get the gal, but she dies from some disease that presses him on to start a non-profit group to help others deal with that crippling disease. Or it could be that story of a boat full of men surviving down to the last one on board. There is success, but at what cost?

In recent headlines, it could be the disastrous hiking trip that forced a young man alone, trapped for seven days by a boulder slide, to consider his life-saving alternatives. He chose to live by hacking off his arm with a blunt pocketknife, losing his arm, but surviving the ordeal.

When interviewing a failure subject, be discreet and understanding. Try to get copies of news articles to help support the findings of the failure without publicly chastising the person who failed. He still has a life to lead, and his friends and family may or may not be aware of his trials during the ordeal you are documenting.

As the story unfolds, your empathy will help weave the emotion into the fabric of his tale. Allow him to suffer, and cry with him if you need to. Make your words tug at the very core of what is human and how we see ourselves in him. Others who read your words will find solace in what you have written.

It may not be the subject you want to interview but it could be the best interview to date that you ever created. It tugs at the very core of what is human and how we see ourselves in him. Survivor stories are not necessarily failures, but they tell depict the chain of events of failure with a heightened sense of accomplishment and survival. It may not be the subject you originally wanted to interview, but it could end up being the best interview you ever create.

Whether your interview is recorded live on camera or printed in a magazine, be sure to get permission to have photos taken and a signed "hold harmless clause," just to help you avoid jumping in front of the emotional rollercoaster they're creating.

Business and company journals, as well as jetliner passenger in-flight magazines, are best known for tapping interview sources for light reading built with heavy emotion. But you probably won't see airline disaster stories on Qantas, or survivor tales aboard any vacation cruise ships, or tales of cross-country trains crashing off a bridge in any railway magazine.

Pathos is for sale; the story must deliver what the readers crave.

The Survival Story

Different levels of survival catch different readers' attentions. If your interview is of a local football hero who survives a car crash that leaves him paralyzed doesn't bring you personal satisfaction, it will to others. The level of intensity is matched by the storytelling. Do you go after the details of a victim of rape once you find out she was only 12? Do you tread carefully around a Vietnam veteran because he has issues with authority and has a history of mental illness since his return to the States? These are questions a more seasoned, investigative, veteran writer and interviewer will tackle head on.

So what about a local hero, a cancer survivor, a business brought out of Chapter 11, or a widowed homemaker in her 60s who became a jet pilot? These are possible survival stories that will get read, help you gain attention as an interviewer, and set you up as an expert in your hometown.

Look for the gems. Everyone has a story to tell. Are the "failure story" and the "survival story" the same thing? Not quite. Where the difference lies is in the circumstances. A survivor will punch through his circumstances—usually brought on by a series of bad luck encounters, poor choices, living conditions, and environment he chooses to change or transform. The failure story is more personal in that it was a failed approach, encounter, or circumstance that happened suddenly. The incident is usually brought on by fate and does not always have a good outcome.

It's Not About You

I was on a tour years ago, walking the "old town" area with 35 other tourists. We were eager to hear about the historical structures and the area's history then get to the galleries and exquisite shopping. Our tour guide had other ideas. He talked about how he had found paradise here; how he loved the weather. Condensed within the 15 minutes of our walking tour, we learned all about his life that wasn't going very far. Our group was tolerant but fidgety. When was he going to start telling us of the colorful history around us? Eventually, after someone reminded him why we were there, he shifted into "tour guide extraordinaire" and fed us what we craved.

Remember, it's not about you.

Each interview is a dance of two moths around a flickering candle flame. You ask and receive. He considers and offers, and then you flirtatiously move around the subject. If you dive into the flame, you stand a chance of burning your wings and spiraling into that waxy pool at the bottom. If you stay too far from your subject, you risk having the candle flame sputter out. If you take over the interview and talk too much, weave tales around only your experiences, or fail to engage your subject to share his expertise, you risk it all. You both lose the light.

However, if you move quickly and dance within the flame but never get burned, both of you will survive and return the next night. Just remember, it's not about you.

~~ 6. TRICKS OF THE TRADE ~~

"Our admiration of fine writing will always be in proportion to its real difficulty and its apparent ease."

~ Charles Caleb Colton

Recalling my early years of interviewing, I started with "Man on the Street" dialogues with students on campus. I would just walk up to them and smile, holding a clipboard propped on my hip. I tried being less intimidating. I slung a camera over my shoulder and tried to keep it against my back. People often recoiled when I shoved a camera in their faces. I wanted to get the best responses by not shocking their minds with camera equipment.

I found that letting them know that a camera shot was in their future would prepare them, allowing for a more relaxed mugshot. Eventually, our campus paper wrote a policy that if you had a public comment to share with the paper, you also had a public photo to share. Students then expected to have a photo taken and even looked forward to it.

Preparation and forewarning are ultimate tools.

It's Okay If You Sweat

Let's say you've just received a call from a booking agent who has a celebrity available for an interview in your home town. You graciously accept the call and write down the date, time, and place. As soon as you hang up, disastrously large sweat stains appear under your arms. Your mind is racing and you have a million things to do before you're ready.

Relax. This is normal. A sign of a conscientious interviewer is the cold sweats prior to the event. Just be glad you did have time to plan.

First Level: Newspaper, Regional News

The first meeting between you and your interviewee should be friendly but matter-of-fact. You should remember to have your writing pad, maybe a clipboard handy with your question pool, a glass of water for each of you, some tissue nearby, and a small tape or digital recorder. Don't forget to use deodorant. Sweat happens.

These are the basics.

Second Level: Magazine or Book

For your second meeting, if you need one, welcome your interviewee in a friendly manner, offer something to drink, allow the person to settle into comfort—since he's already been through the first meeting, he should be more relaxed—then set the chairs or table to get good lighting on your subject for photos, later or during the meeting, depending on the media of choice.

These steps will set the stage for more in-depth reporting, if that is your goal. However, many interviews happen in one setting. Also remind your subject to avoid wearing pinstripes and the color red. No matter our technology, pinstripes can still cause wavy lines on TV monitors, and TV makes the color red look muddy.

Third Level: TV, Web Camera

Make sure you go over the details with your stage manager or production assistant at the studio. Define the colors and placement of the chairs and table. Find a centerpiece, or flowers, or a tasteful stack of books for the table. Have a tissue box nearby. Talk to the assistant about lighting and the best placement of furniture. It's best to be aware of the microphone boom and camera movements above your head. They're distracting but necessary. You may want to inform your interviewee, if they are not accustomed to the camera, not to stare at it but pretend it's not even there. That takes practice.

Just before filming, check everything: hair, makeup, necktie, vest, microphone clip, blouse or shirt buttons—and your notes. If someone pins a microphone to your collar, make sure it's not poking you or slipping into a crevice. No one likes faulty mics. If you are using a teleprompter, be sure to familiarize yourself with it days in advance if you can. Become familiar with your surroundings so you'll look more confident than your subject.

As the camera is rolling, remember that the practice you did years ago is showing now. So indulge in a smile, a small laugh, and a few animated hand gestures. Be as natural as possible. Never sit stiffly. You're allowed to move. Really. Avoid picking at your clothes, pulling on anything, or bouncing your feet or legs, and keep your hands away from your face, especially your nose. Sure, it's a lot to remember, but with practice these pointers will become second nature.

With a web camera, the interview is usually made by an amateur journalist or a marketing consultant, so quality is a larger issue. Make sure that the sound levels are up and balanced. Tighten the shot so you remove distracting backgrounds. Use two camera angles if possible to diminish the amateur single-camera set up. Check to see that the web camera is set at a comfortable distance from your subject's face. No one likes looking up the nose of a stranger.

If you're filming from your office in your home, take a discerning eye at your office décor. Remove personal items: your Star Wars collection on the shelves, a tacky bulletin board, or a refrigerator covered in school art. Compose your staged area so dark walls or shiny, wood paneling can be avoided. Basic setups are listed in First Level. Use them, and think "professional."

If your hands tend to get sweaty, keep a tissue tucked in your palm. Refer to the next chapter for other telling, body-language nuances to avoid. With your tics and affects under control, this interview is a gem. Good job.

Hire an Actor

Spokespersons are just what the name implies: they speak on behalf of another. An actor is hired to become the "face" of the brand or to step in to cover the inadequacies of the original, camera-shy CEO or even the owner. Companies are often famous for hiring the perfect "spokesmodel" or "spokes child" to deliver the brand.

How often have you seen a company's CEO or division supervisor read from a teleprompter for an in-house safety film or promo? I think that's where the term "talking head" originated. How excruciatingly uncomfortable for the audience to suffer through his boring and stiff delivery. In such a case, it would be wise for the company to hire an actor.

If you have a good eye for face and voice recognition, you'll notice the same actors playing different roles in numerous commercials. When they become too recognizable, they either get an offer to be exclusive to that brand, or they get released for a new replacement. Sometimes, the actor's life becomes interwoven with the product he's selling, and the brand could get diminished due to the actor's lifestyle. Even the death of an actor can kill the brand.

Years ago a famous TV actor, Robert Urich, played a suave, tough private eye character on "Spencer For Hire." In real life he contracted pancreatic cancer and had to be dropped from the show. In the interim he took on a dog food commercial. The series of ads showed him getting gaunt, and eventually, bald, due to chemotherapy. Unfortunately for him and the dog food brand, they both declined in health until the dog food company had to fire him in hopes of revitalizing the brand. Mr. Urich died with many fans and dog owners commemorating his toughness to face the public and share his debilitating disease. The brand name, however, was changed in favor of public perception rather than eradicating the man behind the brand.

Actors are often hired to model their hands, feet, smiles, and voices. If you come across an interview situation where the voice of the company is a paid actor, be sure to get time with the true interviewee of the company so your question pool, even though spoken by an actor, will have come to you by way of the real deal. The actor will have his script, and you'll get your quality interview.

Working from Notes

Earlier, I mentioned the practice of working from notes. Preparation for an interview can be as quick as reading through a few news clippings to familiarize yourself or delving into months of research to anticipate as many twists and turns as you might face. When working with a subject wo gives you his notes, be sure there is an agreement in place to cover you, him, and his known associates. Is your project a memoir, a "tell-all" exposé of people currently in the news, or a general information collection, perhaps for a documentary? These issues should be discussed early on and a contract drawn up to delineate these facts.

Whatever it is, you need to make sure the person who is hiring you to put this information together is also allowing you to view, copy, and refer to it during the interview process. Does he have the understanding that the principle topic you cover may uncover other information beyond his notes? How you manage the information during the research phase will determine whether you will stay on as his interviewer, documentary specialist, or ghostwriter.

Everything must be laid on the table.

At the end of the project, will he assume that all of your notes belong to him and his estate? Ask to keep your own notes. Then get it in writing.

Winging It

Although you always hope to have sufficient time to prepare, there will be situations where you don't have the time to do much preplanning. In such cases, winging it is a possibility. I say possible because, as a professional, you should have been taking notes prior to your interviews. Even if the actual interview comes earlier than expected, taking and keeping notes while interviewing will benefit you.

Winging it subjects you to a variety of problems regarding liability, libel, slander, misrepresentation, and erroneous reporting. If you don't have any notes, then I highly recommend a tape recording of your interview as a backup plan.

Even a spontaneous interview should be supported by notes, a camera rolling, or a tape of the event. Besides, your professional image goes a long way if you can stay professional sounding and looking during the entire process. A polished presentation will generate more good feedback for other projects to come.

~~ 7. FOLLOW THE TRENDS ~~

"Every great work of art has two faces, one toward its own time and one toward the future, toward eternity."

~ Daniel Barenboim

I can't even recall all of the advancements we are seeing in technology today. Not only are changes making us adapt in our everyday lives, but so are significant changes in how we conduct interviews. You could argue the point that nothing has changed in the interview process itself; a person still speaks to another person and gathers information to share with others. The premise will continue. How we collect, save, share, store, and entertain—well, that could be old news by the time you read this page.

Technology: The Ever-Changing Frontier

When Captain James T. Kirk, of the spaceship known as *Enterprise*, first stood at the console of the deck and flipped open his personal communicator, history was born. Well, first the dang thing had to be invented, but needless to say, the communicator was the first leap into long-distance. wireless conversations and … interviews.

Today, we know those "communicators" as cellular phones. Each phone has tucked within it the capability of email, voice recording, photography, video cam, and music playback. And don't even get me started on apps for detecting if you turned off your lights before you left for work this morning. No doubt there are other technologies being invented as we get closer to teleporting and holographic capabilities.

The race is on.

Many of us are not keeping up with all the new gizmos, so I will let that go. I will, however, share that the simplified process of capturing voice on a digital device is much easier than dealing with the miles of 8-track tape or mini cassettes of 20 years ago. Gone are the days of lugging a 20-pound video camera over your shoulder. The ease of safely storing an interview session is now encapsulated in a little flash drive no bigger than a Lego block ... remember those?

What you need to know are the basics of managing your equipment. Become the know-it-all of your personal collection of devices. Keep the manuals and chargers handy and batteries in ample supply. Dead batteries are embarrassing. You may have to face your own troubleshooting to keep your tools ready for use. And taking the equipment with you will require you to have a suitcase to carry them in or individual soft packs to tuck into every crevice of your baggage, carry-on, or jacket. Bottom line: be prepared, and never assume someone else will have the exact charger or batteries you'll need for your cell, camera, voice recorder, etc.

Catching Those Tricky Airwaves

The fear of being interviewed can be lessened, to an extent, by sitting in your favorite overstuffed chair or locking the door of your home office. I don't mean avoiding it altogether, but rather, facing a microphone remotely while enjoying the comforts of your personal surroundings.

Let's imagine a syndicated radio personality has called you for an interview about your new book. The tables have turned. You are now the subject. The major benefits of having a taped or MP3 copy of your interview will save you from hiring a professional to interview you for your PR package. You'll get better insight as to how an interviewer feels with a microphone thrust into his face, and the practice will help your public appearances.

Here are some great preparatory notes from marketing manager Scott Lorenz, President of Westwind Communications.

33 RADIO INTERVIEW TIPS FOR AUTHORS

by Scott Lorenz

You've landed the radio interview and it's time to get ready to actually do it. Now what?

As a book-marketing expert and publicist, I have booked my clients on thousands of radio interviews. Here's a list of tips I give to my clients prior to their interviews. Keep this helpful list of interview tips nearby and you'll be glad you did.

1. Go to a quiet room in your home or office; be sure staff and/or family know you are on a radio interview and cannot be interrupted.

2. Turn off other phones, cell phones and anything else that could create background noise, including air conditioners and the radio, etc.

3. Have a glass of water nearby; there's nothing worse than dry mouth on a radio interview.

4. Disable call waiting: dial *(star)70 and then call the studio number. This disables call waiting for the duration of the phone call. As soon as you hang up, it should be reactivated.

5. Be on time. Call the station exactly at the time they tell you, or be at your phone waiting if the station is going to call you.

6. Use a land line phone for best quality. Some stations won't allow a cell phone interview. If it's not possible to reach a land line then use a cell phone in a stationary location and not while you are rolling down the road, as the reception could be interrupted mid-interview.

7. Do not use a speakerphone or a headset; again, it's about good sound quality.

8. Be self-assured. Remember, you know your topic inside and out. Be confident in your ability.

9. Smile, smile, smile, whether on radio or TV—SMILE. You'll feel better, and for TV you'll look better too.

10. Put some pizzazz and energy into your voice. Try standing while you speak to liven things up a little.

11. Research the show and tailor your message accordingly. Just Google the host's name and station and check out their web site. Is it a national audience or a small town in Ohio? What is their format? Is it News/Talk, NPR or Classic Rock or something else? You need to know.

12. Know exactly how much time you will have on the air as a guest, three minutes or 30 minutes ... so you can tailor your answers to the time allotted.

13. Practice your sound bites—out loud before the interview. Communicate your main points succinctly. Practice this out loud.

14. Be informative and entertaining without directly pushing your book, product, or service. Make the audience "want more."

15. A kind word about the host can go a long way. It's good manners and good business.

16. A person's name is sweet music to them so commit to memory or jot down the name of the host and use it throughout the interview. When taking calls, use the names of callers, too.

17. Be prepared for negative comments, from the host or listeners.

18. Be careful not to slide into techno-babble, jargon, or acronyms that few know about.

19. Never "talk down" to your audience.

20. Be respectful of the host because everybody starts someplace. Today they're interviewing you from a college radio station; in a few years they could be a nationally syndicated host.

21. Don't oversell. Remember you are on the air to provide useful information to the listening audience. If you are an author or selling something, limit yourself to two mentions of the book, product, or service. You must

make it interesting without the commercialism. It takes finesse but you can do it. Oftentimes the host will do this for you and you won't need to mention it.

22. Think of a radio interview as an intimate conversation with a friend and not a conversation with thousands.

23. Radio interviews require verbal answers, not head nodding or uh-huh utterances. Hand gestures don't count in radio either.

24. Radio will often use interviews live and later cut them up for use throughout the day, giving you more airplay. So keep your answer to a 10- to 20-second sound bite. You can say a lot in that amount of time and then you don't sound like you are babbling on. Don't go on more than a minute without taking a break.

25. Don't just answer questions. Tell listeners something you want them to know, something they wouldn't know unless they were tuned in, with the promise of more of the same when they buy the product or come see you.

26. Have three key messages. Short, not sermons. Sometimes the host opens the door, other times you have to answer a question and segue to a key message. A compelling message will have the host asking for more. Usually, people can get in two key messages; the pros can get three. But even if you get in only one, you get a big return for the time invested.

27. Lazy hosts open with a lame: "Thanks for being here." Boom! Give a 15 - 20 second summary message. If the host introduces you with a question, be polite, deliver your summary message, and then answer the

question. "Thanks, (use name), for the opportunity to talk about ... Now, to your question (name, and continue) ..."

28. Maintain a positive attitude. Be as genuine as possible and transparent. Don't fake enthusiasm or sincerity. If you're in a bad mood, cancel the interview. Don't pretend to know stuff you don't.

29. Re-read the press release or pitch that got you into this great booking, since the host is going to be using that as a starting point. Often a book publicist such as myself will tie into a breaking news event that relates to your expertise. Be aware of that tie-in.

30. After the interview, write a thank-you note. Since so few people do this, you'll really stand out from the crowd. Most importantly, you may get invited back.

31. Whether the interview is live or taped-live, if you stumble or flub up, just keep going. Often what you perceived as a mistake, the listeners won't even notice.

32. Ask for an MP3 format of the recording before the interview. Often, if you ask ahead of time, the producer will record the interview and then you can use it on your website. Be sure to listen to it later and critique your performance.

33. Ask for a testimonial. Often, that MP3 will arrive with a note from the host saying how much they enjoyed the interview or that "Scott Lorenz was a great interview, he really kept our audience engaged," or "the phones rang off the hook when Scott Lorenz was being interviewed." You can use those testimonials in future pitches and on your website, blog etc.

As a book marketing firm, we'll prepare questions for our author clients ahead of time and include those in our press kits emailed to the stations. Oftentimes, the radio host will read those questions right in order. Other times they refer to our questions and include some of them. We do this to help the host in case they've not had a chance to read the book, which is often the case.

Make sure you know your own material inside and out and are comfortable with everything in it. You are the author of the book or the press release. and they'll ask you, "What did you mean about this or that?" You need to have the answer. You don't want any surprises.

The bottom line, RELAX, you'll do fine. The butterflies you're feeling are what will drive you to do your best. Just follow these helpful tips and you'll be a *radio interview star*!

Scott Lorenz is President of Westwind Communications, a public relations and marketing firm that has a special knack for working with individuals and entrepreneurs to help them get all the publicity they deserve and more. Lorenz has handled public relations and marketing for numerous authors, doctors, lawyers, inventors, and entrepreneurs. As a book marketing expert, Lorenz is called upon by top execs and bestselling authors to promote their books. Learn more about Westwind Communications' book marketing approach at http://www.westwindcos.com/book or contact Lorenz at scottlorenz@westwindcos.com or by phone at 734-667-2090.

I wish to thank Scott for allowing this special glimpse into radio PR preparations. So many behind-the-scenes strategies are not aired for the public. This way you'll have a better insight as a new author and a better on-air product to keep for your personal PR package.

Podcasts, Webcasts, and Skype

With all this new technology come the enhancements of reading an interview or viewing a podcast on an iPad-style mobile device or cellphone. Live-action interviews can now be enjoyed on a number of handheld devices through website software at an even greater number of coffee shops. To take it one step further, a live person-to-person interview can be conducted via *Skype*, a service changing how businesses develop international relationships without ever having to leave the office … or the bedroom, for that matter.

In each of these media, the basics of etiquette, professional courtesy, and the ability to offer compelling trustworthiness are still strong attributes of a good interviewer. More than ever before, the recording ability, broadcast, and ease of storage today must be addressed with the use of a written contract. Impromptu interviews are everywhere. Tapping into a million-plus on-air YouTube recordings muddies the free-for-all attitudes of the younger set of readers and viewers who now expect instant action and gratification.

So let's look at the benefits of this newest age of technology:

Wherever you go and however you record your interviews, you should be highly aware of the business of doing business. You'll need to protect yourself as a business owner much more than the average brick-and-mortar store. The reasons are many, but the proof is in the way businesses are conducted over today's Internet. We need to be vigilant in realizing other folks like to sue for no reason, like to steal with abandon, and like to take over ideas and identities without thinking of the consequences.

By building on your reputation and what you've already learned so far, it would be in your best interest to carefully plan how to protect your basic assets. And in doing that, prepare for ways to grow your assets, develop more products, and diversify the brand of services you may offer.

By building on written agreements, you may launch your interviews as collateral materials for your business. You can establish an archive of interview articles for sale on your website. Packaging your materials in CDs, DVDs, and booklets gives you the flexibility many of us never previously had. You can easily compile the articles into a book form for future sales. You'll be able to offer workshops on your topic of expertise and promote coaching for others who wish to do what you do.

Early on in your interview development, be sure to ask for permission to use a portion of an interview in a news article or content marketing paper before you sell it. It's the only competent way. Lawyers are more vigilant to catch plagiarism since it is so widespread. Cover yourself with contracts. Simply ask for permission directly from the author or presenter you wish to use in interview materials or books. Once permission is granted, make a file of these agreements and include how you chose to use the materials.

Because information, including interviews, is "shared" across continents, it's only natural that you would want to protect what's yours. Study the terms of service on many websites that control their website materials. Design and develop strong Terms of Service and Privacy Policy documents for your own business and then post them on your website. If you do come across someone who has taken your interviews for personal gain, contact a copyrights lawyer for advice.

These following items are important to have:

- ➢ A written contract document for each interview you wish to develop beyond the basics
- ➢ A Terms of Service document
- ➢ A Privacy Policy document on file and on your web site

- A Permission to Publish document to file in resources
- Any supporting documentation, letters, emails, etc. that give you permission to print or record
- Any book contracts from creating an online e-Book, case study, or self-published works, including booklets and traditionally published books

Laws must be followed in order to keep intellectual property and rights in their place. Don't let this part of your business regimen fall to the wayside.

Blogging and Social Media

We've come a long way from diaries and handwritten letters. Even the U.S. Postal Service is suffering from these electronic growing pains which threaten the commerce of a government-subsidized distribution system. Is the complete shutdown of the mail delivery system a reality? We won't know for some time, but in any case, there are more emails and blog posts per day than any surface mail intended for a quick read from a loved one.

Remember that you can be everywhere without being anyone. You can hide away in the most remote—although Wi-Fi-enabled— location, and yet be an international celebrity overnight. Most worldwide audience connections are spontaneous. Many individuals become "one" in a community of voyeuristic entrepreneurs. In some cases, you could say that social media, with its implied terms of social conduct and loose rules of etiquette, has helped to rein in some of the craziness. But because everyone has access to everything, not one of us is alone. What we say and do today will be forever archived somewhere in cyberspace.

With that in mind, I encourage you to wear your business face at all times. A blog post is not the place to rake someone over the coals. Refrain from engaging in petty complaints launched against your local cleaners for ruining a shirt or skirt. Is it really worth the black eye of a personal comment being splattered across the Internet in the form of a viral venting? Don't become a "troll." You can't take back an attack.

On the reverse side of that thought, if someone attacks you or your work, and uses the Internet to air his grievance, don't allow him to take you down. Be considerate when dealing with complaints. You can face the problem head on, attempt to resolve it with diplomacy and tact; offering a replacement or money-back return is acceptable.

However, if all is lost, be ready for a full attack. Some of these cyber punks are known for personal onslaughts. They enjoy a good confrontation from the comfort of their overstuffed recliners. Such people are known as "trolls," someone who may start a vicious string of posts or emails directed at you for sheer pleasure … theirs, not yours.

Unfortunately, there's not much you can do but ignore them, delete their rants, or turn them over to the police department's fraud and extortion unit. You'll never be completely safe from trolls, hackers, skimmers, ID thieves, and any number of clever miscreants in the future. By taking precautions now and developing a plan of action to thwart their attacks, you'll be miles ahead of your competition and better able to defend the home front.

~~ 8. THE JOB INTERVIEW ~~

"Regardless of how you feel inside, always try to look like a winner. Even if you are behind, a sustained look of control and confidence can give you a mental edge that results in victory."

~ Arthur Ashe

Most of the time, people conduct their everyday lives in a routine fashion. The rut is a daily regimen that sets their confidence level. If you change up the routine, stress is created. If you change up the routine too much, that stress develops actions to offset the new stress. You start modifying the routine to adjust for this change in emotion until you have successfully embraced the newer modified routine. You have re-established your rut, and life is good … or is it?

When there is something you must do, but have no experience doing, you must jump in with confidence. But how can you be confident, knowing that the next action you take will be stressful and very emotional? It's the motto of exuberant leaders around the world … "act as if you do," and in doing so you have created the action you wanted. You can now re-create that action again and again until it is second nature to you. Your belief has been altered. Those around you see the change and accept it. Now you do too.

Act As If You Do ...

Most interviews are conducted in an office or a conference room. You sit facing the individual or a panel of inquisitors. Lighting is harsh, smiles are more like grimaces, reflecting little humor or warmth, the chairs are hard vinyl or the extreme—overstuffed nests of cotton and buttery leather.

You, on the other hand, are apprehensive, silently sweating, running through preselected answers in your head, and waiting for the clock's hands to reach some indeterminate point when the interview will begin.

No one will be there to hold your hand, but with a bit of practice and a toolkit at your disposal, it may not turn out that badly.

Although library bookshelves are full of titles about surviving a job interview, this does not always mean the best tactics are printed in them. Specialized interview strategies are available, but no one can ace every interview when so many variables abound. Purchase or borrow a few books on the subject of basic career interviews, and you'll find good, general advice.

But why not consider how the person you'll face will be readying his interview? Will he be working from memory? Or working from a list of questions? How much is he sweating? How much does his day pivot on what becomes of your interview?

Prior to the meeting—and to dispel the jitters—get an idea of your competition, if possible. Speak to others in the waiting room. Find out where they're from, how they heard about the opening, how long they've been waiting, and even what position they are applying for. Some idle chatter helps pass the time and builds a bit of recognition that all of you are in the lion's den, waiting for the roar of the crowd.

Generally, three universal factors can affect any person's interview:

1) The person conducting the interview is an agent of his corporation and not necessarily the hiring manager

2) The level of expertise for which the interviewer is scouting is magnified by your verbal aptitude, not

necessarily your written aptitude

3) The day and time of the interview can swing like a pendulum—either in your favor or against

Let's look a bit closer at Number 1 above:

When an interview is scheduled, you may not know who will be tasked with the job. Most managers dread the interview process as much as you do. The weeding-out process may fall on the subordinate assistant, a secretary, or a clerk whose job it will be to trim the list down to five candidates. If your interviewer is from Human Resources, you may bypass several additional interviews. Do your best, because you won't have another chance to shine. However, if this interview is just the beginning of the process, you'll need to consider ways to keep yourself at the "top of the list" for further interviews. You'll want administrators to separate you from the slush pile, and doing that takes passion, drive, and timing.

Unless they tell you, you won't know the level of expertise of your interviewer. Will they dig deep or skim the surface? Are they a department head or just pulled in to fill a review panel? Are they intimate with the needs of the position?

You can often redirect some of the questions by answering their questions but then asking a question that is pertinent to what you need to know. For example, if a question targets your capability to supervise others, but that wasn't indicated in the job opening, you might ask if there is potential to be a supervisor in the first six months. If their response is good, then you may wish to ask another question relating to supervisory duties later in the interview. Don't take control, but be vigilant in looking for opportunities to ask again.

Now let's look at Number 2:

Interviewers are often tired of interrogation. They may have seen several dozen candidates before you. Each day can run into the next. They are searching out the right person for the slot. Too many frogs in the pond and not enough princes have dulled their senses. To get their attention, you'll need to energize their first impressions of you. It's your energy and attitude that could place you at the top of the list.

Remember to appear relaxed. Let's not presume that you will be. Focus on what accomplishments you brought to the last company you worked for. Were sales up because of you? Tell them. Did you enjoy your last position but were squeezed out or laid off? Tell them. You found that, after your disappointment, the opportunity to move into a better and more prestigious firm was what you really wanted. Stay upbeat. Stay optimistic. If an opening in this company was what you were waiting for, then let them know.

Remember to look at each of the interviewers. Show interest in each question, and be sure to delay rushing into an answer. Pause and consider prior to speaking. This tactic often lets them know you are poised, confident, and not desperate for the job. Rushing to answer and speaking too fast can mark you as nervous and an immature job seeker.

Body language plays a large part in analyzing the potential new hire. *(See the Body Language chapter, "Lie To Me," that follows.)*

Now on to Number 3:

They may never admit it, but early morning interviews will usually swing in your favor. If you get a choice, go with the earliest time. Their minds are more apt to retain fresh memories at the beginning of the day rather than the end. If you get the afternoon meeting, you're interviewers will have just finished their lunch, and half the day has possibly made them tired or surly. Watch for signs of boredom: yawning, rubbing the back of their necks, fidgeting, playing with a pen or pencil.

Once you see any of these distractions, a simple tactic is to ramp up the game and introduce something of interest to them. You can simply introduce some details they have yet to ask.

Example:

"Maybe this is a good time to show you some of my accomplishments that you might be interested in _____." (insert a letter of recommendation where you excelled in a certain goal, or made profit for the company, where you received a glowing report from your supervisors, any awards or accolades for community service).

Keep your information short and upbeat. Any change in the atmosphere will be better than watching one more person yawn.

One time I was interviewed for a documentation team position. I told them I was a writer and that I wrote pretty much anything from manuals, sales letters, and brochures, ghostwriting an autobiography, and technical writing for radio commercials. I liked the variety.

Then one of the managers asked, "Was that you I read on the restroom wall?"

They all laughed and I quickly answered, "Not today. And not in yours."

That got another laugh from an otherwise risqué type of question. Were they baiting me a bit? I don't know, but I wanted to be sure they knew I could take teasing and could dish it out, too.

It apparently worked. Along with my leadership skills, I stood out from the others and got the job.

Not every interview will go well. Don't blame yourself for it. Your approach to their questions cannot be known until they ask them. All you can do is rise to the occasion and be yourself. Most people can read an overly enthusiastic candidate from a nervous one. By being cool under fire, you'll do better than most.

Remember, this is a give-and-take conversation where your input helps to direct the interview. Use what you've learned so far to help them. They will most likely be working from a script or a list of questions. Many companies now use a scored list of questions, weighing your answers for a total to be tallied at the end of the interview. When each candidate is given the same questions, it provides an even playing field for everyone.

Yet the common denominator is you.

How well you dress and look the part of the position you're seeking to fill will be considered. Keep your "bling" and bangle jewelry at home.

Never interview in shorts or cut-offs, halter tops, or tie-dyed T-shirts.

Never wear a slogan on your shirt or coat.

For ladies, check your makeup and hair in the lobby.

For guys, comb your hair and toss out that wad of gum.

How well prepared are you for the meeting? Do you have work history, samples, letters of reference, etc?

How you act under scrutiny or under pressure to perform in the interview, and whether you carry yourself with confidence, will be measured.

If you tend to have sweaty palms, carry a tissue in your hand to absorb the wetness.

What stand-out training or expertise will you offer the corporation to stay at the top of the A-list?

Once the questions have been answered, the panel of interviewers will usually ask if you have any questions for them. If they don't ask, be sure to tell them you do have questions. This is where you can ask about topics not covered, about perks they've mentioned, and about the working environment, like dress codes or standard rules of the corporation. Sometimes, vacation and health package information will come in a follow-up interview. This is a good sign that you've made the first cut. But it also means you have only two other candidates to beat out.

It would be cruel punishment if a candidate who smokes found out there are no-smoking rules applied inside or outside the corporate buildings. Some working mothers rely on babysitting options in the workplace. Without that service, they may find that babysitters are a premium and not easily found. If you enjoy exercise before or after work, ask about company gyms or jogging paths in the region.

Once the interview concludes, be sure to thank them and, with confidence, shake the hand of each person there. It's also recommended to send a follow-up card to show your interest in the position and to remind them which candidate you were.
In your thank-you card, pick a goal or piece of background material that you talked about and write it in your message. Keep it as short as possible.

Example:

I wish to thank you for conducting a detailed interview with me on Wednesday, July 10. I felt comfortable during that time and appreciate your sense of humor about the writing on the restroom wall.

Sincerely,

Candidate for _____ (insert position here)
Rusty LaGrange
(phone number, just in case they want to contact you quickly)

~~ 9. LIE TO ME ~~

"After a certain number of years, our faces become our biographies. We get to be responsible for our faces."

~ Cynthia Ozick

Without truly realizing the benefit of studying people, I could say I was an early student of Kinesics. I had developed a keen sense of when someone wanted to talk to me of their own volition. Something would trigger that response in me, and I would ask them a few questions. I would study how they tilted their head or flashed their eyes as they gave away secrets. Thirty minutes later we were parting ways, but they had literally entrusted me with personal information that was, to me, truly remarkable. Why did they do that? I never did understand how some people can so easily "give away the farm" and not think beyond the sharing of information.

You've heard the stories before: woman on the bus sits down next to a stranger, and they begin a general conversation to pass the time. Hours later they may exchange phone numbers or addresses. But nothing comes of it until years later when a lawyer finds the woman and explains that she is the sole recipient of an inheritance of over ten million dollars. The guy on the bus was a millionaire who enjoyed her company.

Reading people is an art; understanding them to the deepest meaning and applying it to others is a science.

The Science of Body Language

Do you spin your hair around your finger when you get nervous?

That's a "tell," a little habit that returns over and over again, marking your emotions like the nervous laughter of a man accidently entering a women's restroom. We all have them, and interviewers such as police detectives and review panelists pick up on "tells" like a lie detector test.

Body language, technically known as Kinesics (pronounced: *kin-knee-sicks*) is the modern application of communication and relationships. Because of this, it becomes a valuable asset in all aspects of work and business where it can be physically observed.

Physiognomy (pronounced: *fizzy-ogg-no-me*) is a related concept of studying facial features and expressions that indicate a person's character, nature, or ethnic origin. And with that, follows the study of communications in a confined personal space known as Proxemics (pronounced: *prock-see-micks*).

All these add up to the Science of Body Language; something we use every day. In fact, the popularity of the skill involved actually helped create a TV show called "Lie To Me," starring Tim Roth. Inspired by a real-life behavioral scientist, this FOX TV drama tells the tale of a deception expert who helps uncover the truth for the FBI, local police, law firms, corporations, and individuals. "Dr. Cal Lightman" and his team effectively become human polygraph machines, and no truth can be concealed from them.

Extensive studies have generally revealed that humans learn and evolve with their use of expressions through both nurture and nature. In other words, traits inherited by genes, and direct learning, are applied to mimic others. The use and recognition of certain fundamental facial expressions are now generally accepted to be consistent and genetically determined among all humans, regardless of culture.

However, be aware that some cultures vary in body language from U.S. and European practices. For instance, people from

India may shake their head from side-to-side slowly as they listen intently and agree to the communication. Western cultures would read that as not being receptive to the information. Eye contact can cause contention when Australian aboriginal and black Caribbean cultures meet European and Western cultures. The people of the Caribbean expect their young people not to look at others when being disciplined. This could cause confusion and friction if they were interrogated by police in the U.S. It would come across as a sign of disrespect.

Some cultures are not comfortable when being summoned with the use of a curled finger. It suggests they did something very wrong. In many Arab and Asian cultures, pointing the foot at or toward anyone is rude. To an Arab, a thumbs-up gesture is rude.

Although not everyone is an expert in reading body language, some can judge the basics. It all started when you met your mother and father, learned eye contact, voice recognition, and cues whether you should smile or laugh, pout or cry. And the ultimate personal rewards that go with it.

Some people are innately talented to read all levels of body language. Gamblers in the Old West used their skills to read card play based on the way their opponents handled their cards, their body shifts, and their eye movements. The art of reading a "tell" is used today by law enforcement. A police investigator can read the clues given to him based on the "tells" of a criminal during hours of interrogation.

The profession of Behavioral Analysis is a growing industry, and not just for law enforcement. Some employ professional readers to scan department store patrons, preview jury panelists—like the TV program "Bull," a trained jury selector—and even analyze a potential bride or groom. No longer is a credit check reference the only new premarital tool or that first interview, "weeding out" phase for a new job.

So how does the human body give away its secrets?

First, check out any library, and you'll see an array of books on the subject. My book, however, will only reference the basic tells for your quick review.

Body Parts

The Handshake:

At the first meeting, you step forward and extend your hand for the customary handshake. You notice your interviewee is timid and may have a sweaty palm or perhaps offers you a bone-crushing grip. What we present in a handshake can be perceived as a window to our soul. How do you measure up?

A bone-crusher may show that a person is insecure and trying to overcompensate. But a strong handshake that leaves you feeling bruised could also indicate an overly dominant personality. Consider this the door-opener but not the entire picture.

A palm-down handshake can indicate an expression of dominance, while a palm-up, supporting your hand with his left hand wrapped over yours, indicates support and comfort toward you.

But if the handshake is extended and twisted over the top, a person may be trying to express his dominance or strong will.

The "limp fish" handshake is fairly timid, uncomfortable, and cues to a hesitant personality trait.

The best "palm-to-palm"—and most common contact—expresses an intention of honesty and openness and is considered non-threatening and sincere.

Posture:

An erect posture can be a sign of dominance or confidence. However, a person exhibiting an attempt to stay erect can mark him as a nervous and unconscientious personality who is attempting to project an appearance of confidence. A person slumping through an interview can mean insecurity, guilt, shame, and in some cases, boredom.

Eye Contact:

Using the eyes to flirt, to show interest, or to show fear or worry can be a universal trait. As we begin to meet more people from different countries, their own rules of eye contact are often based on their individual cultures. If you happen to go out of the country, pay close attention to the eyes and how other cultures use them to their advantage. International executives receive coaching on a regular basis when dealing with business culture in a foreign setting. It's an investment in diplomacy.

Direct eye contact, clear and concise, can mean honesty and forthrightness. Other contact can show sexual interest, annoyance, happiness, and pain. Flirting usually consists of bowing the head slightly and lifting the eyes and is often coupled with licking the lips. In an interview situation, flirting is generally detrimental, so avoid rolling your eyes and licking your lips. However, a nervous person tends to lick his lips more often. This is not an exact science, so beware.

Playing with your hair is another sign of nervousness, but it can be alluring to a male or mixed with other attributes that are hard to distinguish. When a woman cups her hand, palm out, then tucks her hair behind her ear, it can be an expression of flirting or showing openness and interest. Nevertheless, it can also mean her hair is in her eyes. Go with the obvious.

Even an avoidance of eye contact, as you race through city

streets to reach your appointment on time, can send the wrong signal to everyone around you. It can show unworthiness, dishonesty, and a flight to hide something illegal. Of course, the cop bearing down on you can confirm anyone's suspicions.

Fodder for Assessment

As you consider reading more body language cues, it may be time to access your own expressions. What emotions do you show during the day? At lunch in a café? At evening meals with others? Do you smile? Do you make appropriate eye contact with people? How do you meet a stranger?

Once you begin enjoying the intricacies of body language, you can start managing your own in a more professional and meaningful way during an interview.

It is also known that a right-brained creative person tends to think by first looking up and away to the left; while a left-brained pragmatic person tends to first look down and away to the right. This can give an employee fodder for assessment.

The Mouth:

If a person covers his mouth while talking, he might be lying. Also, consider that he might be hiding crooked or yellowed teeth, a bad odor, or just embarrassed to smile fully. Hiding the mouth while laughing is a common trait that has no explanation.

A tightening of the upper or lower lip can suggest reconsideration or a fabrication. Pursing the lips often shows concern and even lying. Pulling the upper lip down over the upper teeth in an exaggerated pout that draws the chin downward can mean embarrassment, disbelief, or guilt.

As you recognize common traits, also consider how a person's word usage during these body language unveilings compromises his over-all behavior. Does a wipe of the hand down the face really show deception? Or is it a release of deception? Does the quick wipe of the nose, eyes, or chin show nervousness or covertness?

Job Interview Tips

Next time you are the subject of an interview for a job, you might spend time watching your competition and see if their cues give you a clue to their anxiety, confidence, or subterfuge.

When your name is called, try not to be flustered by items you bring with you. Control or contain them in a purse, tote, or valise. It shows organization preparation, as well as confidence. When your interviewer arrives or you enter the inner office, be sure to make eye contact, raise your eyebrows slightly in acknowledgement, smile naturally, and then shake hands confidently but not too long.

Women: Practice sitting in different chairs so you instinctively know that your choice of crossing your knees will look more professional. Never allow your knees to separate widely. That's a whole other body tell to males. Instead of exposing too much leg, wrap your legs to the side and under, with the shins resting alongside each other. Choose a dress or skirt length that is appropriate but not too short, not too matronly. Some women cross their legs at the ankle, but that can look awkward.

Men: You have it a bit easier when choosing how to sit. Basic sitting structure is to keep your knees together. Although most men don't do this, you can allow your knees to separate, but don't slouch into your "home couch spread." The trick is that if you sit up with a more erect posture, you won't be able to slouch.

During the interview, make good eye contact when listening to show your interest, but don't stare. You can tip your head occasionally to show confidence and consideration. Always avoid rubbing, pulling, and picking at yourself. If more than two interviewers are speaking to you, manage to look at both and give them equal attention. You don't know who has the most influence over hiring you. If something said is funny, allow yourself to laugh, but don't go overboard with loudness or duration. No one enjoys a nervous giggle.

At the conclusion, be sure to end with a firm handshake of all persons present; then and only then, stop to pick up your personal items. Collecting your items first, then having to awkwardly juggle them to manage a handshake, is both clumsy and embarrassing. It can also diffuse any judgment they had placed on your confidence.

Emotional Expressions

We can read the expression of happiness by the combination of eyes, mouth, lift of the eyebrows, and showing of teeth. Those are the common traits learned at an early age. The most common expressions, along with happiness, are sadness, fear, disgust, surprise, and anger.

But what about how the body moves? If a person crosses his arms across his chest, he is signaling a defensiveness and avoidance move. He could also be showing his power stance, ready to take on the world. Scratching the nose can mean he's concealing a lie. A person who talks while rolling or moving his eyes to the right and upward shows he is using his right-brain and functioning with creativity and his feelings. A person who talks while rolling or moving his eyes to the left and downward shows he is using his left-brain and functioning with logical facts and memory.

Generally, when someone smiles, he uses the full range of mouth and lip muscles, plus the wrinkles or creases around the eyes and mouth. Someone who is faking a smile will only use the mouth. A true smile uses over 45 muscles to work properly.

A tight-lipped smile stretches across the face in a straight line with teeth concealed. The smiler is hiding a possible secret or shows a form of rejection. A twisted smile is hard to read, showing mixed feelings on each side of the face. A dropped-jaw smile is usually faked and is practiced. A smile with head tilted and looking up is one full of playfulness, teasing, and coyness. The smiler may also flick their long hair to conceal part of a smile as a modified flirtation.

When you see a bottom lip jutting out, it usually indicates upset feelings; add a quiver for a pre-crying sign, and a pout is easily formed. Drawing down of the mouth corners can also mean the person has tasted something sour or is showing distaste for what he is viewing. A downward pout with teeth showing can mean fear of something grotesque and horrific.

Several cues can be clustered to show tension and anxiety when someone is biting their lower lip, grinding their teeth, chewing gum quickly, or pursing the lips tightly. Oppositely, anyone smoking, sucking at a thumb or finger, chewing on a pen, pencil, or fingernail is using self-comforting techniques, all related to children's needs to be comforted. It can mean they are nervous and need to settle their nerves with a memory or feeling that offered comfort in the past.

Watch for the tongue poke. It can happen subtly. It's often an unconscious gesture of suppression or holding back something as a disapproval or rejection of something negative. It's often accompanied by wrinkling the nose. The tongue poke is not the same as licking the lips.

The hand clamped over the mouth with eyes darting is more

related to immediate shock, especially in youngsters who have a more black-and-white view of life. It shows shock at seeing something embarrassing or witnessing something unspeakable. An extreme version would include the use of both hands.

Gestures viewed more often during an interview include hands that seem to have a mind of their own. You could be lying or perceived to be exaggerating if you touch your nose while speaking. Scratching your nose while speaking, although distracting to others, can mean you are lying or exaggerating. This is often exhibited when recounting an event or incident. If you tend to pinch or rub your nose while listening, it can indicate thoughtfulness, or it could mean you're suppressing thoughts or comments that you would rather not reveal right now.

Please don't pick at your nose in public or while being interviewed. If you have a habit of doing it due to nervousness, take a tissue and stuff it in the palm of your left hand. This can help you focus on the reason you want to be accepted socially during your interview. If extreme habits continue, sit on your wayward hand and hope for the best.

Ear tugging, the iconic signal to loved ones by Carol Burnett after each of her live TV comedy shows, actually indicates indecision and is a self-comforting mechanism to deal with anxiety. Use it only when you earn your own TV show.

When the hand begins to stroke the chin or beard, it's a sign of thoughtfulness. However, when a woman uses her hand to support her chin or side of the face, it can indicate evaluation. Yet, when the body is leaning against the chin or face and becomes nearly horizontal, it shows a lack of focus or even boredom. Propping your chin on your thumb with the index finger pointing up along the face is a universal sign of evaluation.

Neck scratching signifies doubt or disbelief. Repeated neck

rubbing usually means frustration. Hand-clasping your wrist also equates to frustration, as if holding oneself back. Running your hands through your hair is usually a sign of exasperation but, in some instances, can show flirtation when mixed with a grin.

So, there you are. Full of information and afraid to scratch, grin, touch your nose, or roll your eyes.

A student of body language, physiognomy, and proxemics could easily spend a lifetime calculating the true meanings of conversations. It is not a finite science. This is your introduction. Use the information wisely.

~~ 10. AUTHOR, TAKE THE STAGE ~~

"Life cannot defeat a writer who is in love with writing; for life itself is a writer's love until death."

~ Edna Ferber

Wonder where the nerve comes to take the center stage? Can it come from your great grandfather's inclination to do the "soft shoe" in college? Can it be learned like any other discipline? Why do some people get stage fright and allow their brains to shut down in public? And why is it that professional actors admit to having "butterflies" and needing to find a quiet place to vomit before taking the stage?

I know, a lot of questions. In this chapter it's time to face your fears and embrace your Public. If you are a writer, have authored a book, and you plan to sell the book, then speaking to those who want your book will be easy; speaking to those who don't know you or your book will be harder.

Developing a persona helps define how you will present yourself in the public eye and will enable you to define the difference between the writer and the author. Who you are when you get out of bed in the morning is the writer. Who you are when you're marketing and pounding the pavement for sales is the author.

You've come a long way in your journey to be a better writer. Now it's time to look at the author in you.

The Brand

I don't wish to make it sound like you're a simple puppet on the end of many strings, but the case *is* simple. You are fashioned by the perception of others. If you allow someone else to manipulate the strings, you are a puppet. However, if you decide early on that a persona of you is a salesperson and entrepreneur who happens to be an author with books to sell, then you have won half the battle.

Most new authors will sit at a table, with other authors sitting at tables, all selling their books. The standard book sales and "meet & greets" are universal. But how can you stand out from a sea of authors? By being a person with a singular goal—"branding" your difference.

Are you a clean-shaven man in your thirties who has written a children's book? Take that difference and make it a benefit to those who are considering reading your book to their children. You must have some insight that prompted you to choose your genre. Explore that and promote the aspects that are different in you.

Are you an 80-ish grandmother who is writing for the first time? Take that detail and explain how you lost interest in children's books on the library shelves and thought you could produce a better one to read to your grandchildren. Tell your audience you wished to produce a legacy book that your children's children will be proud of.

Are you a writer of romance? Do you love the genre so much that you see endearing qualities in so many stories? You want to bring out the best in love and romance that seems to be perpetually buried in smut and lust. It's a strong and competitive genre. Get your prospective buyers to listen to your passion for passion.

Are you a retired professional who can hand down 30 years of good, solid information to a world craving for insight? Do your days of past experiences go hand in hand with the world's quest for retro subjects? Is there a current trend that you can be a go-to person for, reliving your glory days? How will you show today's students that "older folks" like you still have knowledge to share that will impact their future?

The Book Buyer and Sales Etiquette

By selecting several key aspects about you and what you write about, you'll have a much better grasp of how positioning yourself in front of book buyers can increase sales. You'll gain recognition by the way you dress, design your table top, the colors you choose, and the marketing materials you provide.

Things that distract a book buyer may not be the things that distract you. So to be up on your game, you'll need to pretend to be your prospective buyer. As you set up your booth, take a look around. Are you competing with other authors and are their tabletops of high quality?

If you are not in a Book Fair, but find yourself in a regional open-air market or swap meet, scan around and see what your competition is. Do you have hawkers at every corner? Is there a long line of children standing in front of the cotton candy machine? Will your attempt to talk to prospective book buyers be washed out by the loudspeaker? These are all aspects of your sales environment. You'll need to up your game if the environment is noisy, or remain more sedate if the room is quiet.

Let's look at your presentation, starting with the table top:

Do you have a specific color theme for your displays? Research has proven that more females purchase books and allow color to lead them.

Do you have a tablecloth that is free of wrinkles, good quality, and nearly touches the floor? Female purchasers are drawn to rich colors or bright hues.

Select a heavier material like a brocade or velour that gives the look of velvet.

Drab "cammo" cotton doesn't work unless you're selling a military-themed book.

Are your marketing materials aligned squarely on the table or fanned out? Many people who see a jumble of papers and free gifts lying on the table are hesitant to grab anything unless they are clear on your intentions. Place small tent cards on the table, saying: "Free" or "Please Take One."

Be sure to keep your personal items put away. Store things under your table to keep surfaces clear. Your books, bookmarks, flyers, CDs, and other items should be well-marked and priced. Many authors bring their folding table, chair, book stands, and other equipment in a rolling cart. These can be stashed away under the long, flowing skirt of a tablecloth.

Using clear Plexiglas displays for anchoring books is a good device. Wall hangings attached behind your booth can attract shoppers who scan across all surfaces before moving along. Encourage their eyes to linger on large graphics, titles, and blocks of color. If you have the option to choose a booth with a backdrop, take it. A backdrop offers more "eye candy" for the perusing shopper.

Being friendly and striking up a conversation should become easy to you. As your confidence grows, you'll be able to make eye contact, move around your booth area with confidence, and feel comfortable as you hand out bookmarks and business cards like a seasoned professional.

While you sell your books, be careful not to be too aggressive in your selling posture. A buyer can tell when something interests him. If you approach a prospective buyer and pressure him to make a choice, his choice may be to walk away and avoid a face-off.

Who Are You?

The author who performs in his selling suit can't afford to be sloppy, vulgar, smoking, or talking too loudly. An author who believes in his product should jump into the role of bookseller. You may not agree with many of my observations, but the public has a strong opinion about everything. Why not be ready for them and present as professional a display as possible. It's a reflection of who you are.

It's best to conform enough to be genial, dress appropriately enough to appeal to the majority, and state your sales pitch with authority. You don't need to be a used car salesman; rather you should balance your performance with knowledge, esteem, and a sprinkle of panache.

Once the sales party is over, you can return to being a writer … hiding in your den …or strolling on the beach. Just be comfortable in the knowledge that you have given good thought to the overall presentation that you display to your public. They are the ones holding your future in their hands.

~~ 11. PACKAGED TO SELL ~~

*"You can never return from where you came
but you can look back and see what brought you here."*

~ George Farber

It seems like each time we engage in conversation, the potential to gather informative insights is all around us. The act of conversing with another person is technically an interview, casual but usually filled with interesting tidbits. In fact, as you become more knowledgeable about drawing out pertinent information, you'll find conversational interviews are everywhere.

It's how you act on them that will determine how you collect the data. Will you flesh out a story for your local paper? Glean some wisdom from an octogenarian who wishes to share her colorful past? Do you have a school project that has the potential for an interview or two that will enhance your overall package and raise your grade? Are you sitting at your computer's blank screen, hoping an idea will come to you for your next blog post?

For instance, if your interest is in travel, and you find photography less intimidating than most, becoming a travel writer may suit you. Do you always take a camera or phone equipped with a camera on every trip to town?

To help you visualize the benefits of staying alert to new locations, here is a friend and colleague, Mike Foley, who has offered help to hundreds of up-and-coming authors and travel writers. Now in retirement, he has hosted several annual writing workshops and hosted writing workshops on board cruise ships, as well. Now *that's* a vacation package.

Mike Foley also offered a free writer's e-newsletter, *Writer's Edge*, highlighting a specific topic each month. He is a former and now retired editor of *Dream Merchant Magazine* and author of more than 750 published stories and articles. He also taught fiction and nonfiction writing in the extension program at University of California, Riverside. Since 1986, he has operated the Writer's Review critique service, helping hundreds of aspiring writers improve their fiction and nonfiction projects.

I first met Mike in 2001 in my regional writing support group—*L.V. Writers' Ink*—when we were searching for guest speakers who liked small groups. After becoming our group's annual speaker for nearly 11 years, Mike was eager to offer advice here.

Travel Every day

by Mike Foley

Now that spring is finally here, many of us have begun having thoughts of warmer summer months and travel. And, indeed for writers, travel is often a necessity, either for researching a particular setting that you'll use in a fiction novel or in gathering research and doing interviews for a nonfiction travel article where you'll actually be writing about the real-life place you're visiting.

Although you can often research a place and write about it without actually visiting the place (I've done this), most of us understand that there's really no substitute for travel. During time spent in a particular locale, you grasp the subtle qualities of a place, something you simply can't get from standard library or online research. So, whenever possible, I do suggest that you visit and research the places that will play a part in your writing.

"But," you might say, "the economy has been terrible lately. How am I supposed to do any sort of traveling when my budget won't allow it?"

Good question. In past columns of *Writer's Edge*, I've discussed ways to research a place without actually visiting it. But now I'd like to expand your thinking a bit. I'd like you to begin traveling as part of your everyday life. Once you're a writer, you'll probably always be a writer, with lots of story and article ideas regularly bubbling inside you. With that in mind, every place you visit becomes a possible setting for a story or a possible nonfiction article or book. Ideas are everywhere, yet I know many people who still don't take advantage of that fact.

I'm suggesting that you become a "traveling writer," even if you're only going to the supermarket to pick up a few items. You never know what you're going to see, what might be in the environment that will spark a story idea. And so, you need to be ready to capture that idea when it strikes you. Otherwise, it will float by and eventually disappear. You might wind up kicking yourself later because you can't recall the necessary detail to create the piece you had in mind.

So you need to expand your concept of writing to include everyday travel. To become a "traveling writer," you'll need to carry some essential tools.

A New Attitude—For most of us, the world is divided into things that are "interesting" or "not interesting," those things that may or may not be worthy of our attention. An everyday traveling writer sees everything as a possibility. It isn't a question of what's worthy of our attention, it's a question of what we wish to write. We begin with the attitude that we could write about anything we see—ANYTHING. And we can write about it in a compelling way. Once you've accepted that notion, it becomes a question of what you'd like to work on.

A couple having an argument in the supermarket might spark an idea for characters in a short story. Or a person begging for gas money at a local convenience store might spark ideas for articles on gas prices or how economic struggles affect specific individuals. Once you begin looking at life as a buffet of writing possibilities, you'll be surprised at how many ideas you get ... and how many of them are viable.

Willingness—When you're out in the world, you might see something that conjures up an idea. But you might still need more. For example, you might see a man on a sidewalk, selling crafts from a makeshift cart. Instantly, you have an idea for a character or a possible profile article. But you need to know more. You need to know a bit about the person, how they came to be doing this particular thing, and what drives them to continue. And to get what you need, there's no substitute for talking to the person.

Most people might glance at the vendor and then move on. Some might even buy something from this person and then move along without giving him another thought. But the "traveling writer" will stop and engage the person in conversation. To do this, you'll need a willingness to approach people, a willingness to introduce yourself as a writer, a willingness to listen and ask questions. In most cases, that willingness will bring you a new human connection, time spent with a new person, one who may prove fascinating. That's one of the perks of being a writer.

Note Method—Over the years, I've encouraged writers to carry a small notebook and a pen. This gives you the flexibility to take notes or jot down your ideas as they occur to you. Today, there are additional methods that may work well for you. Smart phones can be good for note taking, as well as tablet-sized computers. These electronics will only get better and more convenient. There's no right or wrong way to take notes and organize your information. Find a method that's comfortable for you and then use it regularly.

Camera—If a place strikes you in an emotional way or if it seems like a setting you could possibly use in a story, take a photograph. When you view the photo later on, it can often help you revisit the thoughts and feelings you first experienced there. And that can be valuable when describing the place in your story.

The camera is even more important for nonfiction, where photos can accompany articles or books and support the material in a strong way. If writing fiction, a quick snap with a mobile cellphone is probably all you need to remind you of the place. For nonfiction, I strongly suggest that you carry a small point-and-shoot digital camera that will give you higher quality photos. The better quality photos can accompany your work and attract editors. My son, Ryan, carries a camera and snapped a few pictures of a midnight accident on a snowy road here in Big Bear, California. The next day he sold two of those shots to the local newspaper, which appreciated the higher quality. A camera is an essential tool for the "traveling writer."

The above suggestions won't really take up loads of time, and monetary investments are relatively small. But they will certainly open up new possibilities for your writing. So begin looking at your everyday life as a series of travel opportunities, conversations, and interviews, revealing options for your future work.

~~ 12. THE GIFT IN YOUR HAND ~~

*"You can never return from where you came
but you can look back and see what brought you here."*

~ George Farber

The latest trend that is changing how we look at our world is made of instant news captured on cellphones. With this shift in instantaneous recordings comes the lack of filtering, the lack of cause and effect, and the lack of balanced reporting. It's alarming how one video can be the eye witness, accuser, arrester, prosecutor, and judge prior to the "criminal" being given due process of law. Justice is not only blind, she's not wearing her earbuds either.

The term "fake news" is infiltrating the Internet and social media to the degree that news sources and newscasting companies have to work much harder to earn and verify their position among the consumers who expect detailed reporting. Competing with "man on the street" reports from amateur videographers is like handing a badge to the first guy who got off the stagecoach. Just because you captured news on your cellphone does not make your coverage competent.

Caught on tape, as it used to called, is now caught on video. Nearly every person across the nation owns a cellphone and can track an incident faster and much sooner than the legitimate reporter. Where it once took several hours to gather the news, resource and vet the information, write it and broadcast it on TV, is can now happen in minutes.

The faster that information is shared by means of TV, video, live action shows, or cellphone, the less that information hits the press in a timely manner. This is generally, in my opinion, why the typical old-school newspaper media is taking such a hit at the newsstands. By the time the paper product is out on the streets, much of its contents is considered old news. Older readers will still need to touch and feel it, but younger readers are fine with instant access to the news on their personal devices.

The role a reporter plays hinges on several points, the first being reputation. Working to keep your reputation intact is based on handling the news with utmost professionalism. Factual details and fleshing out the story are crucial to this centuries' old profession, as well as meeting your deadline. Even if your story is pulled for unknown reasons, you should be satisfied in knowing that you offered your best work. That's what reporting is all about.

In the flurry of fake news, consumers and readers are suddenly jolted with the fact that "what you see is not what you get." The modified video is not true action, the clips of cellphone video don't show what led up to the incident, the faked attempts to be an Internet celebrity tarnishing the reputation of someone else are all instances of a video-crazed population seeking justice.

Once the dust settles, and the frenzy of amateur videographers subsides, the truth of public information and the role the professional reporter must adhere to will be the turning points for mass media news. The gift is in your hand.

Among it all will be the steadfast journalist with a microphone, calling out questions, interviewing a celebrity, catching the latest details on the structure fire, collecting the resources that create the in-depth profile. And for them, the tool of choice will be the recorded details captured through the microphone.

The Next Step is You

I wrote this book with the intention of breaking down the barrier between the microphone and the interviewee. I see so many people who show such adverse reactions to a microphone thrust in their face. I bet that in time, with a new generation of interviewers out in public with their microphones, and with the mobility of cell phones, the horror in the public's eye will diminish. It's a "selfie" world out there.

We have such diverse ways of capturing and recording information today that soon something new will replace the obnoxious, bulky, fuzzy-covered, traditional microphone. It may be a pencil-thin wand, a fiber optic lapel pin, even a telepathic implant of some sort that can be turned on or off. Well, at least I hope it will have an off button. Until then, just remember that a microphone is not the muzzle of a gun.

~~ BONUS ~~

The Gift in Your Hand: Microphone Etiquette

These tips are offered by my good friend, author, and book editor, Jenny Margotta, who has presented several small seminars on the topic to new writers and expert authors.

A positive way to help a person talk to you as you gather information — whether for resource material or from a relative you're interviewing — is to put them at ease. A microphone is often stared at like a cobra, a battle axe, or even the muzzle of a gun. Here are some tips to help you conduct a session with a good outcome.

When Conducting an Interview:

Know What You Want. Preparing yourself with a list of questions ahead of time will make you appear less anxious. How you respond and act often affects how your interviewees respond. Use a clipboard or a small notebook with your microphone or tape recorder. Always ask permission to interview and record your subject so they are sure why they are being interviewed. See if they want a copy of your interview for their family records.

Prepare Your Tools. Take your microphone, extra batteries, the charge unit, extra charge lines, several pens, and a camera if you need one. Dead batteries are a bane of a failed interview. A dry pen is a second one. If you use your cell phone as a camera and recorder, be sure you can charge it before and after the interview session. Be comfortable with your personal equipment; it establishes more comfort with the interviewee. Bring your reading glasses. Practice preparing and using your tools.

Set the Stage. Find a comfortable place with a chair and a table. Place a box of tissues and a glass of water at hand. If in the subject's home, ask to sit at the kitchen table so you both have enough room to work and talk. If you meet in public, find a nook where you can speak without too much distraction. A coffeehouse is a good location unless the coffee-crowd chatter fills the shop. A study room in a library is also quiet enough and a neutral place.

Tame Your Wandering Feet. Don't allow your feet to wander and don't bounce your leg during the interview. The more you fidget—like tapping your pen—the more your subject will follow your movements rather than listening to what you have to say. It's best to stay still, slow down, and project a professional persona.

A Microphone or Your Own Voice. When addressing a person with diminished hearing, a microphone is a necessary tool for them to fully understand your questions. Also consider that a small portable PA system, used at low volume, can enhance understanding as well. Learn how to use it wisely. Hold the mike close to your face but *not in front of it*. It should just about touch your chin—well below mouth level. This is the voice angle. Once in place, *don't let it wander*.

For your interviewee, you must control the mike if you find the subject has a very soft or quavering voice. If you have a lapel mike that can be attached to your interviewee, this might be the best way to gather your information. Clip the lapel mike to material to the right or left of their mouth and below their chin. You can also add a comment to the recording to bookmark highlights.

~~ BONUS ~~

Microphone 101

As with all technical tools, it's best to understand a bit more about how the microphone works. Today, mikes come in all sizes and shapes. The typical handheld mike, whether corded or cordless, should have a sliding, ON/OFF button on its handle. Take time to practice with the button, because when you are in front of an audience, a mike failure is usually caused by one of two things: your finger accidently turns it off or the batteries die.

A microphone collects the vocal tones in a specific area as a person is speaking. When you hold a mike, it must be close enough to gather the tones clearly—so they do not sound distorted—yet far enough to not lose the volume of the voice.

This imagined area is shaped like a wedge. It starts below your nose and down to an angle at your chin. It's as wide as the mike is sensitive to the voice. This varies a bit. Calculating the distance the mike should be held from your mouth is based on the length of your thumb.

To test this, hold the mike in your hand and stick your thumb out. Place your thumb on your chin then adjust the height of the mike head below your nose—at your lip level. Never touch the mike to your lips. The tonal quality should have depth, timbre, and volume, enhancing your voice yet keeping it normal. It should broadcast your voice without distortion.

Once you hold and balance the mike to find the "sweet spot" for your voice, that position will be a cornerstone to a good microphone delivery for your eager audience. Practice with your own mike. If possible, practice with whatever microphone is handed to you. With practice, finding the "sweet spot" will become second nature. You want to look comfortable and casual when using it so it becomes nearly invisible to your audience.

Tabletop Mics:

A tabletop mic used at a desk or table is very sensitive to motion. Bumping the table, tapping with a pencil, or any other interruption will cause it to vibrate, jump, or squeal. Amateur radio operators use tabletop mikes for hands-free operations so they can take notes or dial-in a signal on their radios.

Lapel or Lavalier Mics:

A lapel-style or lavalier is a tiny mike that can be clipped to clothing at the neckline of a dress, a collar, or lapel, or even hidden away—as long as the mike can pick up a clear voice. This style is very beneficial to use for people who are overly sensitive to having a mike in their face. With the mike tucked out of sight, they seem to relax more. However, the mike needs a "pick up," a small adapter that sends the voice signal to a potable speaker system or, in the case of a stage presentation, a large public address system with mixer capability.

PA Systems:

If you're using a small, personal PA system to enhance your presentations, be sure to test and practice with the connections between the wireless microphone to the pick-up and the PA links. Several switches are used to aid in turning on each of the components. Many systems have small indication lights that are on when each unit is working. Double check the connections and lights. Another reason to practice.

Many sound systems are practical, affordable, and of better quality than some larger systems used to be. Check with an electronics store or ask others who have portable systems that they use. The broadcasting quality has much to do with the frequency levels that allow you to speak to a small indoor group or to an outdoor venue with traffic noise, wind, and lack of filtering where other voices are filling the airwaves.

~~ NOTES ~~

~~ REFERENCES ~~

Michael Senoff, "Hard to Find Interviews;" online resources web site: www.hardtofindinterviews.com

Scott Lorenz is President of Westwind Communications, a public relations and marketing firm. http://www.westwindcos.com/book or contact Lorenz at scottlorenz@westwindcos.com or by phone at 734-667-2090

Mike Foley, former e-newsletter creator, Writer's Edge, highlighting a specific topic each month. He is a former editor of *Dream Merchant Magazine* and author of more than 750 published stories and articles. He has taught fiction and nonfiction writing in the extension program at University of California, Riverside. Article is copyrighted ©2012

California Writers Club, a non-profit association of writers and authors who are perfecting their craft through support programs, critique groups, and inspiration. The club boasts 22 chapters statewide. If you don't live in California, check the Internet for a writer's association near you. If none exists, start one.

~~ ABOUT THE AUTHOR ~~

Rusty LaGrange is an avid writer, proofreader, freelance marketing consultant, ghostwriter, and blogger. After thirty years in the Mojave Desert, she finds daily events to be entertaining and intriguing at her Rusty Bucket Ranch in Lucerne Valley.

Her love of journalism and graphic arts, coupled with her creative style, gives readers a refreshing and entertaining read. She first published as a ghostwriter for WWII-veteran Anthony Pasqualetti's life story—*Born to Survive—Will to Live*.

Find out more about Rusty at www.aFlairForWords.com and numerous blogging sites, as well as the new blogging community at www.HighDesertBlogging.com

www.ingramcontent.com/pod-product-compliance
Lightning Source LLC
Chambersburg PA
CBHW060900170526
45158CB00001B/428